Wandering Heart Trilogy: A Gay Man's Journey

Eighty-Five Years in the Life of a Gay Man

Book Three (revised)
Nearing Home
(includes Book Three: Harbors)

John Loomis, M.D.

John Loomis, M.D.

WANDERING HEART TRILOGY: A GAY MAN'S JOURNEY
BOOK THREE(revised): NEARING HOME

Library of Congress Control Number: 2019904621

ISBN: 9781797741079

Published by Wandering Heart Publications
New York, NY

Other books by the same author

Wandering Heart Trilogy
Eighty-Five Years in the Life of a Gay Man

Book One: The Search (2010)
Book Two: Lost Hearts (2012)
Book Three: Harbors (2018)
Book Three (Revised): Nearing Home (2019)
(includes Book Three: Harbors)

Contents

When the Wolfsbane Blooms

Even a man who is pure at heart
And says his prayers by night
May become a wolf when
The wolfsbane blooms
And the moon is full and bright.

John Loomis, M.D.

Introduction

This is the third of three volumes of my memoir, *Wandering Heart*. The first volume (*The Search*) described my early years and young-adult life from 1933 (birth) to 1952 (age nineteen). Volume 2 (*Lost Hearts*) covered the years 1952 to 1983 (age forty-nine) and told of my professional and business lives and of several (somewhat) successful or disappointing relationships. Not knowing how else to proceed after one of these personal disappointments, I kept moving forward on a conventional course, which I expected of myself. Other people in general neither helped nor hindered my progress, and I felt myself to be alone. This suited me very well, as I was afraid of people and involvements with them and saw an unattached state as the easiest and most pleasant condition from which to cope with life. The development of alcoholism and recurrent depressions made the road more difficult.

Book Three (*Harbors*) covers 1983 (age forty-nine) onward.

Generally, I was internally driven to seek out, or to try to find, happy romantic/sexual relationships, but these mostly eventually turned into unhappy romantic relationships, and then I had to start over looking for a happy one. After years of looking and hoping, I finally found more contentment.

The death of my father in 1964 and my mother in 1966 caused major turning points in my careers. I was already a practicing psychotherapist but now had to take on the management of the family oil field service business, for which I was almost completely unprepared and which required much difficult work and decisions. Much to my surprise, I was able to make a success of this. This was the cause of mild self-satisfaction. My shyness and standoffish attitude were very helpful in running the business, which saved me from being misled by the hordes of advice and/or scam artists who saw me as a newly arrived lamb for their slaughter. Later on, this same attitude acted as a detriment to success, both business and personal. Not ideal, but it was the best I could do. At the same time, I continued my office-based psychotherapy practice until 1975.

Casa de Palmas Hotel, McAllen, Texas

One evening in March 1979, while cruising in a gay bar hoping to meet someone interesting, I met a young man who was to become an almost-fatal obsession and love object. Bert was about twenty-five, a blond Adonis, charming and intelligent. I was forty-six. We very soon developed a close and passionate relationship. Payment for services was part of our relationship from its start.

Unfortunately, Bert had a severe heroin addiction, with the frequent addition of cocaine and angel dust. I was able to refrain from joining him in this practice, in spite of his repeated invitations and urgings to experience what he described as ecstatic experiences. I had learned from my own substance-abuse recovery (alcohol) that these ecstatic experiences were unlikely and that dead-end suffering was more likely. I usually replied to his offers, "Thanks very much, Bert. I'm sure the heroin and angel dust experiences would be

6

wonderful, but I already have too many problems, and I don't think I can handle any more." The truth was that I was not tempted to join him. When he was using his drugs, Bert looked like he was miserable and stupefied, not ecstatic, so he was not a positive endorsement for drug abuse. I had personally seen the effects of drug addictions and knew the usual expected trajectory.

San Antonio, Texas, about 1960

A major burglary at my country house occurred in early 1983. The police traced this back to Bert and a prominent New York art dealer who had bought my stolen art from Bert.

The police in New York, Connecticut, and Miami became involved, along with another major art gallery in New York. This almost unbelievable event led to and necessitated the breaking up of my relationship with Bert.

After the breakup, I was devastated and only very slowly began to recover.

As I proceeded through life, I met many dear and interesting people and encountered many happy and/or challenging situations and opportunities. Stable love began to seem like a possibility.

Author and friend, New York City, 2010s

Thanks to many unusual, unlikely, or strange experiences, I came to believe that there is much more richness to our lives than could fit comfortably within conventional views.

Although I have been advised to omit any mention or description of highly unlikely, psychic, or supernatural experiences in this memoir, I decided to include some of them as strictly phenomenological descriptions without pushing or denying any particular explanations as to what these experiences "really" were. Much in life is mysterious and/or unexplained or unexplainable.

Author's study, New York City

Author's old dog, Valentine, on terrace, New York City)

Author in New Zealand

Looking into the Past

In the course of preparing this manuscript, I showed it to several friends for their comments. They all asked the same question: "You say this is your memoir. How does it happen that some of the chapters concern matters that happened before you were born? For instance, the chapter 'Twilight in Lübeck, 1673' is set in the years 1635 to 1713, three hundred years before you were born, yet it reads just as if you were reporting a current event. Also, 'Havana after Midnight' begins in 1902 and concerns a famous Cuban composer and a lady who had died in 1882 in Paris and who is now visiting him twenty years later. And the details of the Russian imperial family, who were murdered in 1918, seem very present in your account." I was not alive on earth at any of these times. So how could I include these events in my memoirs? How did I "know" what was happening then? I learned these things gradually, one at a time of course.

10

I believe we live at the intersection or the junction of a number of realities-- a multiverse as it is sometimes called.

After my father died, I sometimes wondered, "Where is he?" Eventually, I came to believe that this was not a meaningful question in that universe where he now existed.

Where is happiness? How much does Mona Lisa weigh? Kant wrote of the "categories of the understanding," and we know that there are things we cannot understand because our minds have no apparatus for dealing with them. You cannot train a jet plane to dance on the stage like one of the Rockettes. You cannot fry an egg on the wind. Many kinds of reality just don't intersect (or so it seems to me). So, in the land of death, "*Where*" has no place on the stage.

Down through the centuries, philosophers have been pondering these questions. Alfred North Whitehead wrote, "A thing is where its effects are." The airplane that flies overhead and which you see and hear, also exists in your ear, your brain, your memory, in the past, and in many other realms of reality, including in the future, and perhaps in a negative, replicating universe. In a somewhat different view of reality, the Dalai Lama said, "Phenomena may have functionality, but lack any intrinsic reality." What does a scam artist peddle? His goods may have powerful functionality without possessing the least scrap of reality, intrinsic or otherwise; but the resulting misery seems inescapably real. Sometimes I think our realities are like a deck of cards, fanned out nicely to show all their different faces. Existential thought would maintain that choosing one of the cards would promote its intrinsic reality and would commit us to live with that kind of reality.

Sometimes I have found myself in situations radically different from anything I had experienced before. To sit quietly and watch is often very instructive, and radically new material may enter our psyches. To experience this is, in my opinion, worth noting. The great American philosopher, Charles Santiago Sanders Peirce, maintained that there are three kinds of logic, which he called, "Induction, Deduction, and Abduction." He meant by *Abduction*, a kind of logic by which new ideas or new material can be generated or pulled away from material already in existence. Where do new ideas come from? And how is it done? What happens? This is cousin to pulling a rabbit from a hat.

Something like this has happened to me a number of times, and I have included some of these experiences here.

Here is what I do when I want to experiment in this realm:

I hold one hand in front of my face, perhaps twelve inches away from my eyes. The fingers are pointing downward, and are slightly spread. I look fixedly at the tip of my index finger. In my visual field I can see the rest of my hand. Without shifting my gaze, I direct my attention to the tip of my middle finger for a few moments, perhaps sixty seconds. Then I shift attention again to give attention to the tip of my ring finger for sixty seconds. And then again to the tip of my little finger for sixty seconds. And finally I shift attention to the tip of my thumb for sixty seconds. Blink, look around, and rest my eyes for one or two minutes.

Then shift your gaze to stare at the tip of another finger. Without shifting your gaze, direct your attention to the tip of each of your fingers, for about sixty seconds for each finger. Rest for about sixty seconds.

Then hold your other hand in front of your face, again about twelve inches from your eyes. Point the fingers downwards, again slightly spread. Repeat the above attentional procedure.

The point of these exercises is to develop your awareness of other parts of your visual fields in addition to the central part of the visual fields.

You may begin to notice that there are almost subliminal movements on the edges of your visual fields. Eventually try to observe these movements clearly without shifting your gaze.

Try to be expectant and accepting of what these movements might be. The movements may eventually coalesce into coherent images or scenes. This is what I did prior to seeing the scenes of Havana, of Lübeck, and of the Russian episodes.

What is the nature of the reality of these scenes? They do not seem to me to share the nature of dreams or fantasies. I revisited each of these scenes several times, with slight changes in their appearances, just as there may be slight changes in the appearances of friends when you revisit them. Eventually I began to hear low voices of the characters speaking to each other. They never spoke directly to me, nor did I speak to them.

If you decide to try this maneuver, I would suggest that you try not to touch or move anything you may see in your scenes. Neither should you try to speak to any of the characters, but you should answer any questions they might ask you.

The scene "We Visit a Grand Duchess" includes a character, the Grand Duchess Maria Pavlovna of Mecklenburg, who specifically spoke to us, asked us a question, and invited us to respond. We responded to her for her benefit, not for our own. This is sometimes called "soul retrieval" and is not really an intended matter of our exploration.

I have used this method to explore a number of other scenes, equally interesting to me, and if you decide to use this technique, be slow and deliberate and prudent; use common sense. The characters may request your assistance; you must make your own decision as to what to reply.

As in the previous volumes, all persons, experiences, and conversations are reported as accurately as possible—as accurately as my memory permits. I saw what I remember, and I remember what I have seen.

However, there is the question of what I have called orphan memories. A memory may have once belonged to someone. But in the course of time that person may have died, leaving the memory an orphan. These orphan memories are like little puppies, crying and wishing for a home, and they may possess considerable energy. Occasionally a vivid memory would suddenly implant itself in my mind with no historical antecedent that I knew, usually in a highly charged situation.

Related concerns involved memories or visions of events that had never taken place and memories of events that have not taken place yet (as in answers to questions that have, as of yet, not been asked) or which will never take place.

We all constantly stand at the crossroads of many possibilities or potentialities. When we move on the road to actualize one possibility, we put the other possibilities into storage where they remain, perhaps indefinitely or even forever. We remember where we were, but we also remember where we might have been. When we are in New York, we may clearly remember what it was like to be in Chicago, or we may remember our tenth birthday party. These events

13

and places remain and persist in a special realm, real but not exactly like our everyday realities.

Sutton Place, New York City, 2000s

We can visit this realm in our memory vehicles. Sometimes these memory vehicles get out of our conscious control and take us against our wills to painful places in the past and are reluctant to return us to our present time. Sometimes these past places are more beautiful than we know in everyday life, and sometimes they are more horrible.

Our special vehicles can also move through time, both backward and forward, and we can learn things that we think are mostly inaccessible to us. I have spent so much time in realms of imagination, fantasy, alternate locations, and alternate eras that I can recognize their special kinds of realities and powers.

Some of these explorations will be described later in this book.

Liverpool – the Beatles lived here

Sutton Place, New York City, 2000s

There are many more realities than the ones in which we spend most of our time and energy, but I would not recommend trying to spend much time in those places unless there is a serious good reason to visit there. They have their own rules that we do not know and that may be very difficult and painful to accommodate. We need a guide if we visit these places.

Volumes 1 and 2 are written in a linear manner, as the events recounted were generally consecutive and had considerable connection and onward momentum. However, the last forty years of my life have unfolded in a different way. Concerning Volume 3 (revised) *Nearing Home*, to try to connect these more recent events in a linear narrative account would be very difficult and not particularly appropriate. Various aspects of my life, such as managing the business, miscellaneous health problems (some of them significant), piano playing and music, friendships and other personal relationships, memories, insights, and a variety of psychic experiences often did not have much essential connection to one another, so I decided to just present them as individual matters in a patchwork, but the boundaries and connections will be plain enough.

Author at home with a cold

Meeting my current partner and spouse of more than thirty years has changed my life enormously for the better. He has been an unfailing source of good advice, practicality, cheerfulness, strength, and encouragement. This relationship was off to a somewhat rocky beginning, as detailed later, but we have both worked to make the relationship better and better. We were legally married at the New York City Hall on July 21, 2014.

There are no fictitious or composite characters, but the metaphysical natures of some of the characters are not always clear. The question is not, what is the nature of these beings? A better question is, what is the nature of the reality of these beings?

Some changes or omissions of names or locations were made so as to disguise the identities of persons who might wish not to be recognized, but this was done without distorting the story or the meaning. Again, as William James said, "A real difference is a difference that makes a difference."

Author on terrace with hibiscus, New York City

I want to thank all those who helped and encouraged me along the way, especially my parents and my partners, who enabled me to continue living, and I need to apologize to all those, in addition to my parents and my partners, whom I have hurt, usually inadvertently. Also, my thanks to John-Richard Thompson, who greatly helped in the creation of this manuscript and laughed with me at the humorous or outrageous sections.

This book is dedicated to my spouse.

John Loomis
December 15, 2016

Chapter 1

A New Start

In September 1981, about two years before the breakup with Bert, but in one of our increasingly frequent disengagements, I had met a younger man, Steve, very intelligent and attractive and obviously interested in me. We met in the same gay bar where Bert and I had met, and I wondered if this was an omen of some kind. He had heard a good report about me from his roommate, whom I had met in the same bar, the Cowboy, some months before. In those days, many roads started in the Cowboy. Steve was forthright, serious about his work, independent, and a good conversationalist and had a fine curiosity and optimism about life in general.

He was twenty-four, and I was forty-eight—exactly double his age. The age difference didn't make any difference then.

After a couple of meetings with Steve, which had, of course, included exciting physical pleasures, Bert reappeared in my life in his usual captivating guise, and I became enthralled again by him. Steve was somewhat disappointed to see me drifting away but stood by patiently, smiling and waving when we met occasionally by chance in the bar.

The final break with Bert, following police involvement as a result of his burglary of my Danbury house, occurred eighteen months later, in February 1983. That sordid and frightening episode is outlined at the end of volume 2 of this memoir.

By mid-1983, my life was again assuming a semblance of normality, or at least the usual routines were again being followed. I saw friends for dinner; continued to practice the piano; went almost every weekend to Roadside, my beautiful house in Danbury,

19

Connecticut; checked on the business very carefully; talked on the phone with distant friends; and gradually became able again to concentrate on reading, financial concerns, and my usual chores. My emancipation from the fierce obsession with Bert was very slow.

Sutton Place Park, New York City

Steve and I got together occasionally, perhaps every week or two, for an increasingly exciting and pleasurable experience. We fell into the custom of having dinner beforehand, and so the evenings became significant events for me, much more even than the fine frolics that marked the beginning of our relationship.

Not yet recovered from the traumatic experience with Bert, I was not eager to fall in love again, or even to start anything more than a very casual relationship. Months passed by pleasantly, and I began to recover from Bert and feel much better. Steve was always polite, pleasant, reliable, cordial, handsome, interesting, and stimulating to be with—in most ways, the opposite of Bert's lying and unreliable nature (although Bert was always very handsome and often really stimulating to engage with).

20

Author in Copenhagen

Very promising, I thought of Steve. He was always enthusiastic and energetic, which caused me to feel that perhaps I was a desirable partner, at least in the mind of one particular person.

Yet, I was able to rein in my enthusiasm and refrain from letting myself become deeply involved. This was a pleasant, casual relationship, I thought, but I neither craved nor dared to let myself think of anything deeper or more long-lasting.

But something very ominous had appeared on the horizon.

The AIDS epidemic was gathering speed and force and was killing many of my friends and acquaintances. The cause was still unknown, and the social opprobrium was enormous. It seemed this was an always-fatal disease, solely afflicting gay men.

Was it spread by using cocaine? Or amyl nitrite? Or drinking contaminated water?

Or by some other substance?

Was it contracted from toilet seats?

Or by using common eating utensils or drinking glasses?

Or by kissing?

Or touching an AIDS patient?

21

Was it safe to eat from the same dishes used by an AIDS patient, even if the dishes had been thoroughly washed, or even sterilized?

Author's study, New York City

Nothing was known, much was suspected, many theories circulated, and an increasing number of gay men were coming down with the disease, which could be fatal in as few as six weeks from first symptoms. A diagnosis of AIDS was effectively a death sentence. The medical establishment, the government health bureaucracy, and the general public were beginning to be aware that a new and mysterious killer disease was spreading through the gay community. There was very little official interest in the matter, as gay men were expendable; perhaps it was even a bonus that their numbers were being reduced, some secretly thought. The *New York Times* refused to use the name of the disease.

I had two close friends in Connecticut, Alden and his partner, Rolf. One day Rolf showed me an extensive and terrible-looking rash—inflamed, irritated, oozing, and weeping—on his right arm, which he said was poison ivy. I believed him. The condition was so painful that he soon had to consult a physician, who diagnosed shingles, but his case affected five dermatomes (nerve distributions), an almost unheard of extreme case. Rolf was very sick.

Rolf lived with his partner, Alden, at their house at Brookside Farm in Danbury. Alden was Rolf's primary nurse for the first several weeks. Rolf's young friend Joe also helped to take care of him. Joe lived at my house, Roadside, as caretaker, also feeding and looking after my two little wirehaired dachshunds, Delilah and Rover.

Rolf and Joe were often together, had often gone to the gay baths together, and had close physical relationships. They were both quite promiscuous – frequenting bars, back rooms, baths, public toilets, and highway rest stops and picking up sex partners where they could find them. They were together enough to be regarded by those of us who knew them as quasi lovers. Alden didn't seem to care, as he was preoccupied with his new boyfriend, but in addition, he occasionally also had relations with Joe.

Steve on the terrace, Fort Lauderdale

Rolf and Joe particularly liked to go to a gay bathhouse in my neighborhood in New York City. I passed by the place frequently but had never ventured inside. It had a reputation as a somewhat sleazy establishment, with lots of booze, dirt, and rowdy patrons.

After Rolf's severe rash had first appeared, he languished at home for several weeks but didn't improve. In fact, his breathing began to become difficult and labored.

He was moved to the Danbury hospital, where it was found that he had an unusual form of AIDS: leukemia with all types of white cells overgrown and proliferating wildly. These cells had filled up his lungs and made breathing almost impossible. His doctor inserted a breathing tube and put him on oxygen, but even so, it was still too tiring for him to use his clogged and stiffened lungs effectively, so he was put on a respirator. This was so uncomfortable that he was connected to a morphine drip, which was designed to make him more comfortable, although it also made him unconscious.

A week passed with no change in his condition. Because his breathing was done by a machine, no one really knew whether he was fully alive or was only being carried by the machines. An attempt was made to lower the morphine dose to see if he might regain consciousness, but he began to moan loudly and thrash about, appearing to be in tremendous discomfort. The morphine was increased again, and he again became still and remained unconscious and unresponsive.

Rolf's sister, who had been following all these procedures very carefully, finally took action after two more weeks. She was Rolf's closest living relative and so had the legal right to speak for him in making medical decisions. She said to the doctors, "If you don't disconnect all the tubes and machines so we can see if my brother is still living, I will bring an immediate lawsuit against you and this hospital."

This energized the doctors, who reluctantly and slowly detached all the tubes and machines from Rolf's body. His heart was still beating, but he was not breathing on his own and had no electrical brain activity. His heart stopped three minutes later, and Rolf was dead. His ordeal was over.

Rolf had a beautiful funeral service conducted by Alden, who by that time had been ordained as an Episcopalian minister. A large reception was held immediately afterward at the home of Rolf's friend, Freddie Haight, in Litchfield. Freddie's mother was the first cousin of Queen Mother Elizabeth of England, and the reception was attended by many elegantly dressed people. Rolf would have loved the party, as this was the group to whom he had gravitated. Perhaps he was looking on from the next world.

Two years previously, his mother had died, and he had inherited a beautiful emerald ring from her, as well as a large and valuable set of sterling flatware. While Rolf was very sick, Alden had taken these items from Rolf's possession and hidden them at my house. He asked me innocently, "May I keep a few little things with you, since you have a burglar alarm?"

"Sure," I said. "Put them away somewhere safe, but where you can find them." I didn't ask what the items were or why Alden wanted to hide them. His motive became clear later on. He hid the ring and the silverware in my house.

A few weeks after Rolf's death, Rolf's sister asked Alden if he had any idea where the emerald ring was—it was a family heirloom and had great sentimental value.

"Oh, no," Alden said. "I haven't seen it." He went through the same routine with the sterling tableware set.

I was disgusted by his lying and avarice, but he was an old friend. As a priest, I suppose he was able to forgive his own sins, if he recognized that he had any. Some years later, I asked him if he had ever returned the emerald ring and the sterling to their rightful owner—Rolf's sister.

"Of course not," he snapped, not wanting to be bothered with such a trivial question.

Joe had continued visiting Rolf in the hospital all through Rolf's final illness. Joe himself had developed some dark skin lesions, and when they were biopsied, the report came back that they were Kaposi sarcoma. Joe knew this meant he also had AIDS. He tried to tell Rolf about this, but he received this knowledge only on Rolf's last day of life. Rolf was unconscious and so never knew that his friend Joe was just behind him in line to leave this world.

Steve in Germany

I invited Joe to continue to live at Roadside as house watcher and dog caretaker, at his usual salary, for the remaining months of his life. He enjoyed watching his goldfish swim lazily around their bowl, and my two dogs would sit in his room, also watching the goldfish. Joe would sometimes tell me stories of what the fish had said to the dogs and what the dogs had replied. It was quite an inventive and elaborate fantasy—we all enjoyed his dog-fish stories. He and the dogs had always been friendly, and now they were keeping him company as he died.

He was sick for several months, but eventually he had to go to a local hospital and then on to a hospice when he needed more intensive care. He died quietly there. His family was devastated, and all who knew him mourned. He was a sweet, kind boy.

Interestingly, my dogs saw his spirit for several months. They would suddenly rush into the entrance hall where he used to come in while he was still alive, would stand looking up into the air and whining while wagging their tails, and could not be called away from the spot for a while. I feel sure Joe had come for a short visit and that the dogs were happy to see him again.

And so the two friends, Joe and Rolf, died close together.

But previously, Alden had been having sex on a more or less regular basis with Joe, who had already been infected with the HIV virus but showed no symptoms at the time. The sex was in a safe form, so that Alden was not apt to contract the infection. Alden's friends were suspicious and anxious about the possibility that Alden was having sex with Joe. When they asked Alden from time to time whether he was having relations with Joe, Alden always answered, "Oh, no. Certainly not." Lying to his friends about such a life-and-death matter as being exposed to AIDS and possibly passing it on apparently did not bother him.

One of our friends described Alden precisely by saying he was an extreme opportunist. This, combined with his severe avarice, made for a serious character defect in the reverend father. Saintly looking he was too, in his beautiful ecclesiastical lace garments and his large silver cross and chain.

*****

I had been drinking far too much, having more severe hangovers, and was getting frightened by my increasing inability to control my alcohol intake. I felt better after a month's sober trip to Africa with my medical school classmates, but upon returning home, the drinking rapidly progressed again. I talked with Alden about it. He had at that time been in Alcoholics Anonymous for about three years and said he felt much better.

He made the only comment that would have had any effect on me: "If you don't want to drink, go to AA. It will make it easier."

It was the *easier* which sold me on giving AA a chance. The following week, Alden drove into New York and took me to my first AA meeting. He could be genuinely helpful.

The speaker at that meeting was a woman who had a manic-depressive disorder, which she said was kept in check by regular doses of lithium, as prescribed by her physician. One of the other members spoke up, angrily accusing her of using mood-changing chemicals and told her she was dishonest and had no right to speak to the group. I was shocked at this piece of hostile misinformation used as an attack but just stayed quiet. The member needed to think

27

about her own hostile and ignorant bigotry. But, after all, it was my first meeting, and I didn't know the routine regarding speaking up. As time went by, I began to attend more meetings, and on a regular basis too.

One day I noticed a purple spot on the right side of my chest. As Kaposi sarcoma (KS) had been the presenting symptom of many gay men when they came down with AIDS, and as no one yet knew how it was transmitted, I was, of course, worried that the spot might be KS. I made an appointment with a dermatologist I had seen several times before, and he immediately performed a biopsy. When I returned to get the report, he looked serious and ill at ease.

"I'm sorry to tell you, but your biopsy was reported back as Kaposi sarcoma," the doctor said to me.

I sucked in my breath, feeling like I had been punched in the stomach.

"This is a very serious matter," he said.

That was no news to me. I fully realized that I had just been given a death sentence. I must have blanched and looked upset, for the doctor continued, "You will not be alone. We will all be with you at every step. You will never have to be alone with this," he said politely, but he was in no way reassuring or believable. "I want you to see Dr. Flesch, who is a recognized specialist in the treatment of AIDS." He then called his secretary to come into his office. He asked her to make an appointment for me with Dr. Flesch.

When his secretary came into the office, saw me sitting there, and heard the doctor's request, she began to cry softly. She had known me at her previous job as secretary to the veterinarian who had taken care of my dogs for years. We had been on friendly terms there, and she was upset when she realized my diagnosis. A little later, on my way out of the dermatologist's office, I said to her, "Thanks very much for your concern. I have an idea that this situation may improve. Please don't worry." Hers was the only genuine human concern I encountered at either the internist's or the dermatologist's offices.

As I left the dermatologist's office, he said in a pseudo reassuring voice, "We'll be in touch soon."

Of course, I never heard from him again. So much for his promise of support.

The next Monday I was at Dr. Flesch's office at two o'clock in the afternoon.

After introducing ourselves, Dr. Flesch had some administrative-type questions for me: place of birth, date of birth, parents, siblings, etc. He asked about my previous experience with psychiatrists, whom I had consulted several times over the years for depressions. All went well until he asked me my profession.

"Physician," I said.

"Pardon me?" he said.

"I'm a physician—a psychiatrist," I said.

"Oh, you mean you went to medical school and all that kind of thing?" he asked with a sneer and a giggle, obviously finding what he took to be my lie hilarious. I wondered what kind of arrogant nut case I was talking with.

"Yes, that's right," I replied, smiling calmly and inappropriately at him.

"Well, you seem more upset than you should about this information."

I wondered what was a more appropriate reaction after receiving a death sentence—an announcement of a fatal disease apt to kill me in a few months.

We had a brief discussion about treatment. At that time there was no effective treatment for AIDS, and a blood test had not yet been developed. The movie star Rock Hudson had just returned from consulting a physician at a hospital in Paris known for "treating" AIDS patients. His photographs looked terrible, and he died a couple of months later.

"Do you think I should go to Paris to consult Rock Hudson's doctors?"

"Yes," he said. "Why not?" And after a few moments, he added, "I want you to see a good psychiatrist I know, Dr. Phil Snar. He's not like the amateurish types you saw in the past. He happens to be my lover, so I know he is very qualified. Here is his number. Give him a call this afternoon and get started in treatment as soon as you can." Pulling out some paper from his desk drawer, he began to write. "I'm starting the application for you to go on welfare and to qualify for food stamps."

Flabbergasted, I said, "Oh, let's wait awhile to do that. Maybe that won't be necessary." He had never asked me anything about my financial status, which was quite good at that time.

Irritated, he crumpled up the paper and threw it in the corner. "Suit yourself," he snapped. "Come back to see me in two weeks, after you've started treatment with my lover."

I was appalled at the whole interview. His arrogance was only matched by his rudeness.

When I got home that afternoon, I called Dr. Snar's office and scheduled an appointment for the next week, but with some misgivings about the whole procedure of getting started with these "AIDS specialists."

Three days later, I was so uneasy about Dr. Flesch and his referral to his lover, Dr. Snar, that I called Dr. Snar's office and cancelled my initial appointment with him, still five days away. Three weeks later I received a sizeable bill for the nonvisit. Never having seen him, I was not yet his patient, and it was unethical and blatantly greedy for him to send me a bill. Disgusted, I paid the bill and never made another appointment with Dr. Snar, and I never returned to see the arrogant Dr. Flesch. *A close call*, I thought, but fortunately I had escaped the clutches of these money-grubbing hacks.

Another lucky escape!

The next Monday I received a phone call from Corinn, Bert's wife, from Santa Monica. She told me that a week before, Bert had been found dead on the bathroom floor at his niece's house. She implied that the cause was an accidental heroin overdose. This seemed very likely, as he was a severe heroin addict but was otherwise in excellent health. He was forty years old. A young life, filled with beauty, talent, and promise—now suddenly snuffed out. I began to cry briefly, as did Corinn. She said that their son, Hardy, now age eighteen (whom I had known years before as a very young child—a beautiful, small copy of Bert), was planning to visit New York next month. She wanted to know if he could call me and arrange a meeting.

"Yes, of course. I would like very much to meet Hardy," I said, "but I am planning to be away next month. Please tell him to call me, and I hope we can get together."

I never heard from Corinn again, or Hardy. I had always been afraid that Bert might enter my life again and regain his hold over me. Sadly, I was finally relieved of that serious possibility and fear. Thirty years later he is still often in my thoughts, and I remember him with love and sorrow. He was a dark, charismatic star. His image still shines brightly in my memory.

My head was in a spin, having just heard the news that Bert was dead and being told that Hardy was coming to meet me. However, the very serious question of whether I was infected with the HIV virus was still up in the air, and I hoped it could be decided as soon as possible.

I had been consulting a psychiatrist, Dr. Colter Rule, for more than a year for the treatment of a recurrent depression. Dr. Rule was about seventy years old and knew many physicians in New York. In spite of my presumptive diagnosis of AIDS (acquired immune deficiency syndrome), I did not have a very suggestive prior history. I'd had shingles a few years earlier (somewhat unusual in a man in his late forties), but didn't have other common features of early AIDS, like pneumonia, fevers, and other infections.

Dr. Rule referred me to a doctor who was a noted immunologist. He examined me and then said that my story was certainly not typical for AIDS. The specific blood test for AIDS had not yet been developed, but there were some other blood tests that were often abnormal in AIDS patients. He did all these tests, and they were all reported as normal. He said that these normal blood tests would be very unusual in a patient who had AIDS. My only abnormal test was the original biopsy from the dermatologist's office—the thing that got the ball rolling in the first place.

Fortunately, I still had the slides from the biopsies. I contacted my friend Dr. Vicki Curry at Memorial Sloan Kettering (a leading cancer hospital in New York) to ask for her advice. She said she thought the chief of dermatopathology at Sloan Kettering, Dr. Bijan Safai, one of the world's foremost authorities on Kaposi sarcoma (the marker in my case), should look at the slides and offered to take them to him for his examination. She gave him my slides two days later.

The next day Vicki called me to say that Dr. Safai had seen the slides and wanted to discuss the results with me.

Uh-oh, I thought.

When I saw Dr. Safai at his office at Sloan Kettering, I found him to be a middle-aged man, trim, energetic, and intelligent, but patient and kindly. "I looked at your two slides very carefully. They are both almost identical to the microscopic pathology of Kaposi's sarcoma. I can see why someone might think they were Kaposi's. When I looked very carefully again, I saw there was a similar proliferation of small blood vessels, but definitely they were *not* Kaposi's. You have a benign tumor of the small blood vessels. There is no treatment required. It helped a lot that you still had your original slides." He smiled as he gave me back my slides.

I gave a huge sigh of relief and a very heartfelt, "Thank you," to Dr. Safai. This meant that I did not have AIDS.

A few months later, the blood test was developed. With some anxiety, I went for the test and a week later found that the test was reported as negative. So this was another sign that I did not have AIDS. Five years later I had another AIDS blood test, which was again negative. I never told Dr. Flesch or Dr. Snar about the blood tests. I felt, possibly too negatively, that they would be very disappointed that a prospective victim had escaped.

I thought of Edna St. Vincent Millay's poem, "Dirge Without Music":

> *Down, down, down into the darkness of the grave*
> *Gently they go, the beautiful, the tender, the kind;*
> *Quietly they go, the intelligent, the witty, the brave.*
> *I know. But I do not approve. And I am not resigned.*

Life seemed to have a new start. I tried to remember what a friend had told me: "The future is welcoming."

Chapter 2

Departures

In 1995 my partner, Steve, resigned from his New York banking job to go to live in Japan to study the language. He announced this plan to me as a surprise one day, without asking my opinion or reaction. I thought our relationship had broken down and was being discarded. He didn't see it that way, and our relationship persisted. But this unilateral action did serious damage and was only very slowly repaired.

After he had lived in Tokyo for a few months, he told me a studio apartment, just like his own, had become available in his apartment building, which was called the Foyer Monet. It was located in Ikebukuro, one of the busy commercial centers of Tokyo. He asked if I would be interested to rent it, so as to spend some time there—with him, I assumed. As a retired physician, I had the time and freedom to do this, and so I said, "Oh, yes." I wondered why he had asked me to join him, but I looked forward to the adventure of moving to Tokyo.

After I arrived and unpacked in the new little place for the first time, Steve said, "You know I am here for serious study and probably will be very busy with that."

I soon established a schedule of six weeks in Tokyo and then six weeks in New York. It was a hard schedule, as I was jet-lagged for about ten days after each transition, which included fourteen-hour-plus plane flights. About 120 days a year were spent in the distress of jet lag.

33

I felt excited about the move to one of the world's major cities. Living in Tokyo was a challenge. For a while I didn't like the city. There were few street names, for instance, and the language problems, with almost no English signs, were formidable. But I liked the museums and concerts—Tokyo has eleven full-time, functioning symphony orchestras and a multitude of other concerts.

One evening I attended a piano recital at Suntory Hall (Tokyo's premier concert venue) by the eminent Japanese pianist Izumi Tateno, who, unfortunately, had suffered a stroke, incapacitating his right hand. His left hand was unaffected and was as skillful as ever. Tateno was one of the greatest lyrical pianists I had ever heard, although his reputation had never been as great as he deserved. His playing expressed a resolute aloneness, best heard in his performance of Finnish music—the music of the country where he had lived for so many years with his Finnish wife, music in which he had no equal. (All great pianists excel at presentation of the various emotions. Arthur Rubinstein, the greatest pianist I ever heard, for instance, was a master at expressing every possible nuance of yearning.) Four contemporary Japanese composers had written left-hand piano music for Tateno, and the program was entirely devoted to the debuts of these new and interesting works.

At the rather prolonged intermission, there was a stir in the back of the audience, and then a number of serious-looking, well-dressed Japanese gentlemen filed into the hall and took their places, standing around the back of the hall. A large section of the seats had remained empty. There was a ripple in the audience, and then Michiko-Sama, Empress of Japan, escorted by a distinguished-looking older gentleman, entered the auditorium. The audience applauded; the empress smiled and nodded graciously as she took her seat in the reserved empty section. She is said to be an expert pianist and was very attentive to the performance. There was an extra dimension of profundity to Tateno's playing that evening.

When Izumi Tateno appeared, he bowed first to the empress and then to the audience in general. The music was beautifully performed. The empress stayed until the end of the recital. There was something extremely moving about this very elegant and elegiac evening. This was a very special occasion—one of the peaks of my concert going life.

Steve was diligent in his studies, although we often met for dinner. I didn't want to make a nuisance of myself by insisting on too much attention. I had been warned. I didn't know anyone and did not readily make friends or acquaintances; I was almost completely isolated.

Fortunately, I was an alcoholic and a member of Alcoholics Anonymous, and so I was able to attend the English-speaking AA meetings in Tokyo. This was really a lifeboat, and I met some interesting and cordial people, whom I still know today. I attended two or three meetings a week and usually had lunch with the group afterward.

In 1997, after about two years, I had learned to like Tokyo very much. It is wonderful city to live in but is not warmly welcoming to the newcomer.

Steve decided to return to the United States, where he rejoined his old firm. He was soon posted on to London and assigned a good position there, including a very nice apartment. I switched my half-time living arrangement from New York–Tokyo to New York–London and very much enjoyed the new arrangement and living in London—one of the world's most pleasant and interesting cities, where I had visited several times previously as a casual tourist. And the five- to six-hour flight was more manageable.

Just before I left Tokyo for London in 1997, Liz, one of my friends in the program, said, "There's a new American man, gay, who's just moved to Tokyo. He's been in the program ten years and says he doesn't know anyone here. He seems very nice, but a little lonely. Would you be willing to talk to him?"

Of course, I agreed, and a few days later Rick and I had our first lunch together. I found him extremely intelligent and charming, and we had a pleasant conversation. Otherwise, I don't remember much of the lunch, being preoccupied with plans for leaving Japan.
But after two years in London, my friend, Steve, was transferred back to Tokyo (in 1999), still with the same firm, as head of one of their banks there. His career was advancing.

And so the New York–Tokyo routine started again. We had a much larger and nicer apartment near the American Embassy. This time I was more comfortable, having learned my way around Tokyo. This is an inexact remark, as Tokyo has seventeen million people and a huge land area, but being able to recognize a few subway stations and some other locations was a big help.

Rick

I saw Steve at least briefly most days, but I felt somewhat neglected and isolated. Like most expatriates, he worked very hard. When I told him of my feelings, he didn't have much to say. But we soon went on a week's vacation to Sydney, which eased the stress between us and made things more pleasant.

Steve was very practical, efficient, strong, helpful, and effective. Over the years he has helped me enormously in many ways. He expressed his affection in practical action, such as fixing things around the apartment or helping me to fight my battles against bureaucrats.

Later on, as he got more experience with business matters, he was able to help me with those aspects of my life too. He frequently decided to do something special and then followed through, such as bringing food home or helping me with the computer (if I asked).

Crises arose from time to time. For instance, one night I had sudden, intense abdominal pain. As a physician, I had never before seen the onset of severe abdominal pain.

I went through the differential diagnostic possibilities in my mind. Most of them were serious; some were ominous. I didn't know what my problem was, but I was frightened, and so I pounded on the wall between our adjoining apartments. Soon Steve came in to my apartment.

When he came in, he looked worried. "Have you had a heart attack?" he asked.

"I don't think so, but I don't know what this is." I was literally writhing, could not stand up, and could not stay still. A few aspirins hadn't helped, and I had nothing stronger. Many severe pains cause the sufferer to stay very still, but this pain absolutely prevented me from staying still. I could not find a tolerable position, and so I moved constantly.

I continued to writhe and moan. The pain subsided a little for the next hour but then came back twice as bad. I couldn't stand much more of this and knew I couldn't make it to any hospital on my own. I thought of jumping off the terrace but decided to ask for help instead.

I said, "I'm so sorry to be a nuisance, but I can't stand any more pain. I have to go to a hospital, and I'm afraid I can't make it on my own." I felt very embarrassed and guilty about bothering him. I continued to writhe and cry out constantly as the waves of pain grew stronger. We went downstairs, caught a taxi, and went to the Toranomon Hospital near the American Embassy (where it was said that many famous people had died).

After examining me briefly, the pleasant young doctor told me I was constipated, gave me a laxative, and sent me home. I was not convinced this was the root of my trouble, but as it turned out, this was the best possible course of action, much preferable to being hospitalized and perhaps operated on in that hospital. In-patient routines in Japan are somewhat different from US practice, and I was in no condition just then to try to accommodate a new routine.

For the next month, the severe pain came and went, gradually decreasing from 75 percent of the time to 25 percent of the time. I still didn't know what was wrong, but because the pain was often absent, I planned to wait the six weeks for my return to New York to consult my internist.

In spite of the first attack, I made plans to travel alone by Shinkansen (the bullet train) to Kagoshima in the south of Japan and then to Hiroshima on the way back to Tokyo. The pain of the attacks was incapacitating and made it nearly impossible to stand up or to walk. I almost fell in a department store in Kagoshima when a pain attack hit, and in the next few days I had a dozen more attacks in Hiroshima. The waves of severe pain lasted anywhere from one to eight hours each time, and then I experienced about an equal time with no pain at all. In Hiroshima I discovered that the pain was helped slightly by sitting in a tub of warm water. Aspirin was slightly helpful, about like throwing a cup of water on a large house fire. When I returned to Tokyo, Steve told me he had passed his Japanese language proficiency exam, and I congratulated him on this important accomplishment.

When I returned to New York for a short visit in 2003, I visited my internist, who discovered that I had a large kidney stone stuck in the left ureter. This was what had been causing the pain. It took two drastic procedures to remove it. The first procedure was lithotripsy (using strong shock waves aimed at me as I sat in a large tub of water). The intention was for the shock waves to pulverize the stone in place, but this was totally ineffectual in my case, as the stone was too large. The doctor expressed skepticism and irritation with me when I told him I thought the stone was still inside, as if I were malingering. What could I say? Later on, further tests revealed that the stone actually was still inside me and in the same location as before the lithotripsy procedure.

The second procedure, again done in New York about a month later, involved placing a catheter through the left ureter up to the kidney and then inserting a laser through the catheter, so as to be in direct contact with the stone, and blasting or exploding the stone with the laser. This destroyed the stone, and small pieces kept coming out for the next two weeks. They had to be caught by urinating through a fine mesh strainer. The problem was solved. I have not had a recurrence. The pain of a kidney stone fully deserves its hideous reputation. The chance of developing further stones was unknown. This unpleasant episode was resolving.

The next time I returned to Tokyo on my regular schedule, I resumed my Thursday program meetings and was happy to see my old friends. I looked forward to another long visit to Japan.

I had a regular premeeting lunch date every Thursday with an American teacher, a very intelligent man who chaired the Tokyo Writers' Group, which I soon joined, as I was planning to start writing my memoirs. Unfortunately, my friend's work schedule eventually changed, and he told me he could no longer make the Thursday lunches.

Rick and author in Brooklyn, New York City

At the next AA meeting I saw Rick (my new friend from the previous visit to Japan in July) and asked him if he could have lunch with me the following Thursday. He seemed a bit surprised but smiled and said he would be delighted. We made a date to meet at the Harvester Restaurant on the Omotesando (Avenue) the following Thursday at noon. This started a series of weekly meetings that continued over the next three years.

We told each other of our drinking history and our gay history, and this started us on our way to becoming well acquainted. We slowly discovered many interests in common, as well as common knowledge of past historical events. Eventually we came to feel we had known each nother in a past life and began to have an idea of who we had been. We imagined that we had been mother and child in our last life. (He was the mother and I was the child.) I had not treated her properly and felt guilty about my behavior toward her. In that lifetime I had died about ten years before she did.

By now we had not had contact for almost eighty years. We were delighted to be reunited. The fact that many people would find such ideas bizarre did not bother us, although we knew we shouldn't discuss them carelessly. I continued on my regular schedule, going back to New York for a visit every six weeks and then spending six weeks in Tokyo. Sometimes I was sorrowful when leaving Tokyo and seeing Japan disappear behind the horizon, but knew I would be coming back to Tokyo soon.

It was always a pleasure to be with Rick. He smiled and seemed to find my conversation interesting. On the street, if there was a rough stretch, he would put his arm through mine to help steady me, and I could feel his affection for me. This was not an intellectual construct, but an emotional experience.

One day Rick brought along his American partner of ten years, Glenn, a writer who was living in New Zealand but was currently visiting Rick. He was writing a weekly blog, "Moon over Martinborough," about life of young expats in New Zealand, which had been voted New Zealand's best blog. Glenn was handsome, charming, obviously very intelligent, and had a very positive and cheerful outlook.

I asked him to read something I had written, knowing that as a beginning writer I needed help and advice. He returned my piece in about three weeks with extensive and helpful comments. Rick invited me several times to be his guest at his club, the Tokyo American Club, and we continued to become better acquainted. Rick radiated good cheer, which was felt by most who came around him.

One day I gave him a CD of Jorge Bolet playing Cesar Franck's "Prelude, Chorale, and Fugue." He seemed very surprised and touched. A year later he told me that the piece always reminded him of me.

We shared many details of our lives and were struck by how similar some of our experiences had been, including interest in the psychological and psychic aspects of our lives. We were growing fonder of each other and knew our bond was getting stronger.

I felt safe inside the relationship. Strangely, no clinging or dependency developed on either side. I had had so little experience with friendship that I didn't realize I was experiencing the beginnings of a new friendship.

*****

As my permanent departure from Japan came closer, Rick and I talked about how we could maintain our contact. One day while we were having coffee in the Capital Tokyu Hotel close to my Tokyo apartment, Rick looked at me seriously and then spoke of his affection for me. I was tremendously moved and immediately replied, "And I feel the same way."

A barrier had fallen, and we both knew how special the situation was. But now what? We both felt it was unfortunate that we could not have spent more time together as friends during this lifetime. As we parted that afternoon, we both had painful feelings and feared we might be at the end of our relationship just as this happy chapter was opening for us.

Two days later we had a final meeting and tried to make plans to continue our contact, even if only by e-mail and telephone (and later, by Skype). We agreed that the relationship was not and should not be a sexual one. To make the situation even more improbable, Rick was thirty-seven years old; I was seventy. And we were dear friends.

After I left Tokyo in 2005, we talked often by phone, and I returned to Tokyo several times in the next two years for month long visits, staying again at the Prudential Tower apartment. I brought a rollaway bed into the apartment at the Tower of Comfort, as we called the Prudential Tower, so Rick could stay over with me instead of wasting two to three hours a day on the subway commuting from his apartment to his office. We were very happy to spend time together.

We spent hours listening to music from a disc player. As we listened to our favorites, the Cesar Franck piece, Rachmaninoff's second concerto, or Chopin's nocturnes, we continued to get better acquainted.

I had brought a digital piano into the apartment, which I used frequently. Rick often asked me to play the piano, and I enjoyed playing for him as he listened attentively. He particularly liked a little piece by Mussorgsky, "Une larme," and asked me to teach it to him, so we started piano lessons, which we both enjoyed.

At the end of each of my visits to Tokyo, we were melancholy, never knowing when or if we would see each other again.

Rick and Glenn

In 2005, Rick talked of moving to New Zealand, where his partner, Glenn, was now living and working and managing their two pieces of real estate. I encouraged him to make this move, as the long-term work situation in Tokyo for a foreigner was not promising, and also to help in his relationship with Glenn.

He found an equivalent project design and installation job in Wellington. Although he missed his friends and working conditions in Tokyo, he soon settled down in New Zealand and began to make a new life for himself. This move took him even farther away. Wellington is nineteen hours by jet from New York (instead of the fourteen hours from New York to Tokyo), even though only six or seven time zones. We continued to talk by telephone and Skype and to exchange e-mails.

Rick and Glenn bought another piece of residential real estate in Wellington, making three properties, all of which they rented out. They also found a twenty-acre property outside the small town of Martinborough, in the Wairarapa farming and wine-growing region, about forty miles east of Wellington.

Martinborough is very much like Napa, California, was thirty years ago. This fine property lay over a mountain range in one of the wine-growing areas of New Zealand. Rick told me how beautiful it was. He said, "I live in a paradise." He invited me to come for a visit, which I accepted. The property was beautiful, and many kinds of fruit trees, vegetables, and olive trees were thriving, a well as being home to a number of sheep, cows, pigs, and chickens. Sometime previously I had told Steve of the meeting in which Rick and I told each other of our affection. I tried to reassure him that this development did not threaten our relationship.

I told Steve of the reincarnation ideas that Rick and I shared and stressed that we were both recovering alcoholics and had a common bond in AA. Steve was uneasy when he heard all this; fortunately, he eventually came to a toleration of the situation. He didn't know for a long time whether our boat was sinking or only going through a rough patch.

He was not pleased about my plan to visit Rick in New Zealand but eventually came to understand that if he blocked me, it would damage our relationship, so he ended the discussion by buying me a ticket to New Zealand for my Christmas present in 2006. This generous and surprising act perfectly showed his very kind spirit.

Farm in New Zealand

Rick and Glenn on the porch, olive grove in the background

Rick and friend, New Zealand

The past few years had produced an expansion and wonderful unfolding of his psyche. And so I went on this trip in October 2007, which was springtime in New Zealand.

Rick met me at the Wellington airport. It was a very happy reunion with many hugs. We drove over the mountains to his place in Martinborough, which he had named Taha Awa, a Maori term meaning "by the water." Rick and Glenn had a sprawling and comfortable ranch house shielded from the road, beautifully planted with New Zealand shrubs and flowers. It was about ten miles outside town and was at the top of a gentle incline that sloped down to an orchard of several hundred olive trees. There were white wooden fences dividing the property into a number of paddocks.

Beyond the olive orchard were large macrocarpa trees (New Zealand shelter trees) and farther down the hill was a small, clear river that marked the property's back border. Beyond the river were large green hills. Local farmers rented the pastures to graze their sheep and cattle, and this added to the beautiful pastoral scene.

My hosts were very cordial and took me on tours in the vicinity, to see the ocean cliffs and the seal and penguin colonies.

Rick had told Glenn of our feelings for each other, and Glenn commented that we were having "an affair of the heart." He did not show any jealousy or hostility, and I think our openness made the situation easier for all involved.

Rick arranged for himself and me to go for a short tour of the South Island, including the Bay of Many Coves and the city of Christchurch. He then returned to Wellington, and I went on to Queenstown and an overnight cruise on Milford Sound, one of the great sights of the world, before heading back to Martinborough.

My hosts went to work by train to Wellington every day, returning in the evening. We sometimes went to dinner at one of the many fine restaurants in the Wairarapa region. They offered to leave me their car to go exploring while they were in Wellington at work every day, but I declined, as I didn't feel comfortable driving on the left side of the road.

The last night in New Zealand, I treated us all to a hotel stay in Wellington, which they enjoyed.

Friendly pigs in New Zealand

When they left to go to work the next morning, we all said good-bye, and I caught an early afternoon flight to Auckland, changing there to a flight for Los Angeles. After resting there for one day, I traveled back alone to New York As the months passed, we talked of another visit, and this took place in October 2009.

The visit began like the one in 2007. Rick and I made plans for a week's tour of the South Island, visiting Invercargill, Stewart Island, Dunedin, Lake Tekapo, and Christchurch. We rented a car and so were free to explore. We saw the penguins emerge from the sea at sunset and run into their little underground cave homes. We both enjoyed sitting in the confined space of the car and talking at length every day. We took a detour to Nugget Point, a brilliantly scenic place on the east coast. During this trip, barriers kept falling, and we became closer than ever.

While my hosts were away at work in Wellington, I was happy to stay at their house to play the piano and work on my memoirs. Rick and I were both sorry about the approaching end of my visit and gave each other occasional discreet huglets.

The last night there, I took us all into Wellington for an excellent dinner at the Yacht Club, and then we had rooms at the Intercontinental Hotel.

After breakfast the next morning, Glenn went off to work, leaving Rick to say good-bye to me. We sat for a while in a silent and motionless attempt to get our spirits to cheer up. Rick reluctantly left the hotel room. After he left, I rested for a while and then finished packing and left for the Wellington airport. It has always been hard for me to say good-bye.

I entered the airport, checked in, and went to the departure area. As the flight was called, I gave a huge sigh and boarded the airplane.

I was among the first passengers to board. As I approached my seat, a middle-aged Maori woman had already seated herself. She smiled at me as she got up to let me get to my window seat. The other passengers boarded. An older lady, slender, regal, very erect, and with white hair, glanced at my Maori neighbor and me with a smile and took the aisle seat. She pulled out a small book, started to read, and didn't speak until we landed at Auckland an hour later.

Rick and Glenn's house, New Zealand

Author in Hobart, Tasmania

Author in Hobart, Tasmania

My neighbor wanted to talk and said her name was "Gloria, like the angels." It was only her second airplane flight, and she said that she had loved her first one three days before. After a few more pleasantries, the plane taxied out to the runway and had a fine takeoff. As I looked down at the land, the beautiful bay, and the city on the hills so close by (Wellington is one of the world's most beautiful cities), I began to sigh again, trying to suppress any noise and keep my face turned toward the window. Gloria silently slid her left arm through my right arm and kept it there for the complete flight. She began to stroke my arm as she looked at me sympathetically.

In response to her questions, I told her that I had been in New Zealand to visit some very dear friends whom I loved and that I was getting older and feared I might never see them again.

Gloria asked, "How many children do you have?"

"None, and how many do you have?"

"Three—two girls and a boy. They are half grown now, and I am so happy that they are still living with me and my husband. How many children do your friends have?"

"None," I said, as Gloria nodded and smiled. She had already known the answer.

We talked of Maori beliefs about life after death, reincarnation, and telepathy. She was quite comfortable in this discussion and was spontaneous, intelligent, and forthcoming in her remarks.

As the plane began to descend toward Auckland, I again began to sigh, and Gloria comforted me by stroking my arm and smiling gently at me.

The plane landed and taxied to the Auckland airport building. Gloria said, "I've asked my ancestors to go with you today, to help you and protect you until you get home."

As she was standing up, the older lady looked at me intently with a dignified and kindly expression and said, "You could not have been seated in a more appropriate place today. There are no coincidences in life, you know." She looked at me again with radiant eyes and then walked briskly up the aisle.

Gloria hugged me, kissed me tenderly on the side of my face, gave me an angelic smile, and then followed her neighbor up the aisle.

I left the airplane quickly and thought I might see my two companions inside the airport, but they had drawn their cloaks of invisibility around themselves. I believe that perhaps these angels were in the airplane especially for my benefit, and that once we had landed, they no longer needed to manifest their presences.

On the twelve-hour flight to Los Angeles, and then the six-hour flight on to New York the next day, I could sense the invisible guardians accompanying me. Although I continued to sigh from time to time through the rest of the trip, I didn't feel alone or unprotected.

But I was too calm, and wondered if a viper's eye might be watching me.

Tasmanian devil, 2013

Chapter 3

Laura

For the past forty years, a tragic dilemma has been hanging over my thoughts.

In 1972, I was working as an attending psychiatrist at the Converse Clinic, a leading psychiatric hospital on the West Coast. One morning I arrived to find a new patient had been admitted the evening before, and I had been assigned to be her doctor.

Laura was seated on her bed looking dejected. She appeared older than her twenty-five years, was of average height, considerably overweight, and wore a rumpled pajama-like outfit. This was her usual daily outfit, at least for the fat half of her time. Her light auburn hair was unkempt, and stray strands dangled. Her pretty brown eyes were red-rimmed, and I assumed she had been crying. She wore no makeup on her freckled face and no fingernail polish. Sandals without socks showed her chipped toenail polish.

She slumped and kept her head down, her eyes averted. She spoke slowly in a soft, low voice, seemed depressed, and did not volunteer any information. She was polite, quiet, cooperative, appropriate in her behavior, and seemed quite intelligent.

Over the next few days, Laura told me of feeling hopeless about her inability to control her eating. Her weight moved rapidly from one hundred pounds up to two hundred pounds while she was bingeing and then back down to one hundred pounds while she was dieting or fasting. The cycling never stopped; her weight was never stable at any level. The cycles had started when she was about fifteen years old, not long after she had become physically adult. Laura always hung back from dating; she was too preoccupied with her weight and eating.

Her weight cycles had gradually become more extreme in pounds and shorter in duration. Self-induced vomiting and use of diuretics and laxatives had become frequent; Laura realized these could be dangerous, but she couldn't stop. As time passed and her condition became ever more extreme, she became despondent. Laura started checking in to dieting and fasting establishments, both in Europe and in the United States, including two stays of a month each at the Klinik Anslinger in Zurich and also several long stays at the Klinik Buchinger on the Bodensee in Germany.

Eventually she learned of a diet program at a leading hospital on the West Coast under the direction of Dr. Adolph Good, a physician who was a leading expert in weight loss and eating disorders. In early 1969 she checked in to his hospital.

At first she did very well, lost weight (going from 200 pounds down to 110 pounds), felt more in control, seemed less depressed, and was hopeful about her future. After two months, she moved from the hospital to one of the "diet houses," where patients were free to go out but were supposed to take all their meals in the diet house. The meals were mostly rice and a few vegetables. Eventually the patients could have a slightly broader menu, but one still aimed at weight control.

Laura told me of certain restaurants in town that catered to the diet-house patients. These restaurants were quite dark and had booths with wide side panels or curtains to hide the occupants. They featured two-, three-, or four-pound steaks and other gargantuan meals for the diet-house patients, who could gorge while safely hidden from discovery. She described other ways the patients could cheat on their diets, with predictable results.

She began to cheat on her own diet, at first rarely, then occasionally, then frequently. She began to gain weight but would plead innocence and ignorance of the cause. The staff at the hospital knew exactly what was going on. Neither miracles nor spontaneous generation of flesh were considered likely causes of her weight gain.

Laura felt worried and guilty and realized she was slipping. Dr. Good watched his patients carefully, and he saw those who were regaining weight in private consultation. He offered counseling and "special therapy" sessions.

After a few weeks in our hospital, Laura became more trusting and confident in me, and she gave an account of her stay in the diet hospital. She told me what happened in a typical special therapy session. The dialogue is approximate, but the events are described exactly as Laura reported them:

Dr. Good said, "Well, Laura, what's going on? You're gaining weight again."

"Oh, Dr. Good, I don't know. I've been keeping strictly to my diet—the one you prescribed for me. I'm so upset that this is happening—it's so unfair, when I try so hard to make you proud of me."

"You're lying again, Laura. You're a bad girl and a very sick, lying girl too. What are we to do with you?"

"Maybe you could prescribe a different diet or let me have more exercise. Please, Doctor."

"You must be shown where this lying and sneaking food will lead. Come into my treatment room now." Behind Dr. Good's desk was a double door, soundproof and concealed by heavy draperies. The draperies muffled any sound that might escape from the small room on the other side of the door. Dr. Good unlocked the door.

"Oh, no, Doctor. Please don't give me a treatment ... I'll be good from now on ... I promise ... No, please don't."

The doctor looked at his backsliding patient with scorn and anger, took her by both arms, and pulled her into the treatment room, closing the double door firmly behind him. Fastened sturdily to the wall at various levels were iron rings. An examining table also had iron rings attached. There was a hard, straight-backed chair with more iron rings and one large easy chair. A locked cabinet stood against the wall. There were no windows.

"Well, Laura. You know what you have to do. You want to be cooperative, don't you? Or do you want to make me angry so that I might have to expel you from this hospital?"

She slowly took off her pants and her panties, her blouse and her shoes and stockings, but left on her brassiere—just the way Dr. Good liked. She was sobbing quietly.

Dr. Good unlocked the cabinet and removed a set of handcuffs and several whips.

"Okay, Laura. Do you want to be whipped on your front or on your back? Chained high or chained low? It would be best if you participate in your own treatment, so please choose the options you think will be the most effective—the most therapeutic—in helping you."

Slowly Laura turned her back to the room and put her hands part way up the wall, next to two of the iron rings. The doctor quickly snapped the handcuffs on, fastening her hands to the rings.

"Good girl, Laura. You know that for the treatment to be effective, it must overcome your resistance, don't you? I am going to all this trouble because I really love you."

"I know that, Dr. Good. And I really love you too. I love you so much."

The doctor, who had much practice in torturing his patients, skillfully applied his whips to Laura's back so as to cause maximum pain with minimum visible damage. At first slow and moderately energetic, he gradually increased the force and pace of the whipping. Laura tried not to cry out, which made the doctor increasingly angry. He whipped harder and harder so that eventually Laura lost control and began to scream.

"Good. Good," he said, dancing in a frenzy of lust as Laura screamed louder and louder. Suddenly he stopped dancing and whipping. He began to gasp. Laura could hear him pulling up his zipper.

"That's all for today, Laura. I am sure this treatment will prove very helpful to you, don't you agree, dear?" He unlocked the handcuffs, and Laura was free again.

"Oh, yes, Dr. Good," Laura murmured as she dressed herself and quietly left the treatment room and the doctor's office to return to her usual daily activities.

As she finished her account of a special therapy session, she fell silent and stared blankly at the floor for a few minutes.

I was shocked to hear this fiendish story. "Well, Laura, I am really sorry this terrible situation happened to you, especially since you were all alone at the hospital. Was there anyone to help you? Was Dr. Good ever caught and punished?"

"No," she murmured. Laura told me about the rest of her stay there. "I spent eighteen months total at Dr. Good's hospital, and my weight went up and down, as usual. I couldn't get control of the weight situation, and I got more depressed by the month. During one of my mother's visits, I suddenly broke down. I couldn't take it anymore. I told her what had been happening: 'I was one of Dr. Good's favorite patients. If I gained any weight, I would have a session of special therapy. I would be chained to the wall and whipped. He had a secret torture chamber behind his desk. I know of three other patients, also favorites, who received the same special treatments from him. He sometimes whipped his patients.'"

Her mother told me Laura showed her the bruises on her back and thighs and the whip marks on her back. Her mother was horrified but persuaded Laura to introduce her to the other three patients, all young women. Two of them confirmed the story. The third girl refused to say anything or to show any of her own marks, but she did not deny the story either.

Sobbing and gasping, Laura said to her mother, "I want to stay in the hospital. I love Dr. Good. He's the only one who can help me. He's my only chance for a healthy life."

Laura's mother didn't agree and promptly removed her from the hospital and took her home. Her mother considered making a complaint to the hospital or to the State Medical Society but was afraid her fantastic story would not be believed and would only result in a slander suit from this world-renowned weight-control doctor. Proof of her story would be very difficult, if not impossible, to present.

Recuperating at home from Dr. Good's hospital, Laura became even more depressed and hopeless and resumed bingeing. Then came three months at a fasting clinic on the Bodensee in Germany, where she had been before and where she received legitimate, but stringent dietary restriction, combined with acupressure treatments.

Next followed three months of bingeing at her parents' home outside Philadelphia. Then three months in a fasting establishment in Denver, then months of bingeing at home. Then three months at a fasting retreat in upstate Vermont. The pattern went on and on.

When Laura entered the Converse Clinic, her weight was 150 pounds and was on the upward slope of her cycle, having increased from one hundred pounds over the previous eight weeks. She was in good physical health. Gradually she became less depressed, enjoyed talking with the other patients, and entered into the routine of the hospital with a cooperative attitude.

She appreciated being confined in an institution so that she could not wander into restaurants, bakeries, and delis. She commented that San Francisco was a difficult place for a bulimic, as there were so many food/eating places along the street.

Visits from her parents and her brother, Bob, were pleasant for all. Her parents and her brother were genuinely caring and supportive, but they were worried as to how they could help her and confused by the ominous progression of her disease. Well-to-do, they were able to afford the ongoing, very expensive care, not only in Dr. Good's hospital, but also in spas, psychiatric hospitals, the Converse Clinic, and dieting establishments in Europe and the United States.

They would have done anything for her, if only they had known what to do. Her family and I had many conferences concerning various specific problems and also about general principles of trying to promote independence and self-esteem while at the same time being supportive but not coercive or smothering. It was a difficult situation for all of us.

After three months in the Converse Clinic, Laura was considerably improved and was discharged. She went home to her new luxurious apartment, where she lived alone, having recently decided to move away from her parents. She and her parents thought this independence might be good for her.

She and her family decided she would continue her consultations with me in my private office. Laura gradually adopted a living pattern of spending about 75 percent of her time in dieting institutions. The other 25 percent of her time she spent alone in her apartment.

Within the next month, I spent a holiday weekend at a house party in the Hamptons. The other guests were medical people, among whom was a well-known surgeon. At one point, the conversation turned to weight loss and dieting, and I asked the surgeon if he had ever heard of inflicting pain as part of a weight-loss program. "Of course not," he replied, showing irritation.

Taking a chance, I asked him if he had ever heard anything like that said about Dr. Good, the famous diet doctor. "He's one of my best friends. He would never do such a thing. Anyone who says that about him is a goddamned liar, and I would want to punch him right in the nose.!" the surgeon said.

The conversation was finished, but not forgotten.

*****

After Laura left the Converse Clinic, she and I met in my office on a regular schedule twice a week. We discussed problems with her family and matters concerning her life, such as dating, friends, marriage, and a possible career.

Through her parents' and her brother's wide circle of friends, Laura received many invitations to parties, dinners, excursions, dates, concerts, and other events. She turned them all down with a simple, "No, thank you," without explanation or excuses. She had beautiful clothes and jewelry, but only rarely wore them on those infrequent occasions when she was both thin and had some self-esteem.

Laura seemed to trust me, and I felt she was telling the truth as best she saw it. She had a clear, cool eye for the behavior of others. She never appeared to be lying, distorting the facts, or refusing to talk about any subject, except for matters of her weight and diet problems.

She was not interested in going to school or in working. She turned down any suggestions as to the value of developing a more active social life, which currently consisted entirely of seeing her parents and her brother.

Often rudely abrupt in her rejection of my suggestions, she could be so persistently hostile that I lost patience with her. I even felt flashes of anger toward her, which, of course, I did not allow to show. I wondered if this had been the way she provoked Dr. Good to punish her, in order to overcome her resistance to his therapeutic efforts. But I understood, according to Laura, that Dr. Good was a sexual predator whose bad behavior was unprovoked, always inappropriate, and inevitable in relationships with young women patients.

Laura's scornful rejection maneuvers were repetitive destructive features of her relationships with others, even with her parents and brother.

Her mood depended on her eating behavior for the day. When she could remain without food all day, she felt cheerful and said the day was a success. If she ate a regular-sized meal, she thought she was losing control and became panicky. If she binged on food, she would become despondent and say she wanted to kill herself.

We had very little conversation that was not related to food and weight. Even when Laura weighed one hundred pounds and looked emaciated, she said, "I'm a fat pig and need to lose weight." When she was at two hundred pounds, she likewise said, "I'm a fat pig and need to go to a hospital—or, better yet, kill myself."

She made the rounds of her usual spas and fasting places in Colorado, Vermont, Austria, and Switzerland, with occasional stays at other places. She always had success in losing weight in these spas but promptly regained the weight on her return to Philadelphia.

I tried to persuade her to write a guide book to dietary establishments around the world, as she had a tremendous fund of information on the subject, but she refused.

Little by little, Laura became more hopeless, and she began to talk seriously of suicide. About one year after she had left the Converse Clinic, I was able to persuade her and her parents that she should return to the hospital for protection and for treatment of her depression. After six weeks at the clinic, she was more cheerful and hopeful and was discharged.

Laura continued to consult me in my office and visit the spas, with the usual loss and gain cycles. She continued her social isolation. In other words, her situation was not improving. During the next eighteen months, she was slowly getting worse. Complaining of trouble sleeping, she asked me for sleeping pills.

In medical practice there is sometimes a dilemma: Which course of action is apt to be the most helpful? Which course of action is apt to be the most harmful?

It was important to Laura and to the course of the treatment that she should feel I trusted her, while at the same time acknowledging that I knew she was seriously depressed. To refuse her request for sleeping pills might have precipitated her leaving treatment.

Reluctantly, I wrote her a prescription for sleeping pills, but only after she promised that she would not use the medicine I had given her to commit suicide.

We heard of a new medical development that might offer significant help to Laura. Intestinal bypass, a relatively recent surgical treatment for obesity, was becoming known. During the procedure, a section of small intestine is bypassed so as to shorten the food-absorbing pathway. The operation was considered quite serious, and there were numerous possible severe side effects, up to and including death. There were only a few surgeons performing this new procedure.

The bypass was very effective in helping patients to lose weight and keep the weight off. She saw this as a last-chance procedure for her and began a campaign to arrange for the operation. I agreed readily, and so did her family.

However, surgeons at the closest hospital where the operation was performed did not want to proceed on the grounds that her weight was not high enough. They wanted a minimum weight of at least twice the person's normal weight, and Laura at her maximum weight was lacking about ten pounds. They also pointed out that she was able to lose weight by more usual methods of dieting and fasting.

I could not emphasize to the surgeons the point that Laura was hopeless and suicidal about not being able to escape her weight cycle. Her life seemed more or less useless to her. It would have been against her interest for me to mention her idea of suicide, as any emotional instability would have frightened the surgeons away.

But I was able to emphasize that the stress she was under was very harmful to her physical health and that the bypass operation promised the best possibility of returning to a normal lifestyle.

Two of my psychiatric colleagues and I wrote letters supporting the bypass procedure. The surgeons -- arrogant, irritable, and unhelpful -- finally and reluctantly agreed to go ahead. Laura was overjoyed. I had never seen her this way before, and it gave me a glimpse of what she must have been like before her illness so damaged her.

Her parents wavered a bit as the day approached, but Laura was resolutely determined to go on with the procedure and was cheerful and hopeful. The big day arrived, and the operation was done. I visited Laura two days later while she was recovering in the hospital. Although she was in considerable postoperative pain, she was elated and talked of things she wanted to do in the future.

After an intestinal operation is done, the digestive apparatus shuts down, and the patient must be fed intravenously for a few days. When the digestive apparatus begins to function again, liquids and then solid food are gradually introduced. During this time, there is usually a weight loss of about ten pounds, sometimes a little more. Laura lost ten pounds, as expected.

When she was able to eat again, she was in a much better mood and was apparently able to avoid fasting and bingeing. Even so, she slowly began to gain weight, which eventually exceeded her preoperative level. There were no signs of any of the ordinary postoperative features of the procedure, such as digestive difficulties, abdominal distress, or food intolerance. All were concerned at this odd turn of events, especially Laura.

As her weight continued to rise, the surgeons were noncommittal and said she needed to be more careful about her eating. In other words, it was her fault if she did not have a good result from their operation. The operation appeared to have been a failure, totally lacking in benefit.

And so another round of bingeing at home and fasting in the spas began. After almost a year of this familiar routine, Laura again became hopeless and suicidal.

Her internist and I felt that the first operation was not extensive enough—that not enough of her small intestine had been bypassed. According to the literature, this sometimes happened, as the operation was still new and not well standardized. Laura pushed for a second, more extensive operation, and her internist, her parents, her brother, and I all agreed.

We went through the same routine to convince the reluctant surgeons to do a second, more radical operation. This time it was more difficult to persuade them, as there was now the added factor that their first operation had been a failure, with some implied criticism of their judgment and/or surgical technique. They were among the very few experts in the new bypass procedure, and they worked at a leading hospital. It did not occur to any of us to switch to another of the few surgeons experienced in performing this procedure.

Never did the surgeons express any compassion or even concern with Laura's problems or her situation. But they finally agreed to do another, more extensive operation. Laura was again cheerful and hopeful.

The same postoperative course occurred, again completely devoid of any of the common postoperative features. Laura lost ten pounds while still in the hospital, but then her weight slowly started to increase. She was soon approaching two hundred pounds again. She became more and more depressed and seriously suicidal. She gave me three of her books—an ominous sign, as if to say she would not need them in the future. She refused to reenter Converse Clinic. I called her mother, who was away at their summer house, and suggested that we needed to persuade, or even coerce, Laura into hospitalization, as she was very close to committing suicide.

Her mother replied, "Nothing has seemed to help much, and I don't think a forced hospitalization would be of any use. But I am planning to fly up in two days to talk with her."

When her mother called to say she was coming to visit in two days, Laura told her, "I don't want you to come up. You're not welcome just now. And if you come, you will find something you wouldn't want to see."

Laura told me of her conversation with her mother. She also said that over the past year she had seen various internists and had gathered a large supply of sleeping pills. I called her mother again, but again could not persuade her to act to try to save her daughter.

I was surprised that her mother was so reluctant to intervene, even though I had told her that Laura was on the brink of suicide. Without her mother's agreement, or against her wishes, there was no possibility that I could arrange involuntary hospitalization for more than a few days. Laura would be able to pull herself together to appear normal, and I felt sure she would deny suicidal intent, or even depression, and so could arrange for her own release.

At our final session, Laura gave me two more of her books, and at the end of the hour, she held my hand, gave me a long serious look, and said good-bye. I told her that she should call me at any time if she were worried or upset and that I expected to see her at our next regular meeting in three days.

* * * * *

Two days later my phone rang. It was Laura's mother, crying but coherent. She said she had arrived at Laura's apartment to find her dead, lying in her bed with pinkish froth dried on her mouth. There was an empty bottle of sleeping pills nearby. There was no farewell note from Laura, a surprising but no doubt deliberate oversight, a hostile gesture toward her parents. I told her mother to call the police and said they would come right away to help.

The police were called. Laura's body was removed, and the required autopsy was performed. The day after the autopsy, her body was cremated, and her ashes were scattered. There was no funeral or memorial service. Her parents did not offer any rationale for this omission, and I did not have the heart to question them about it.

Those who asked were told that Laura had died of a sudden perforated stomach ulcer. The surgeons called after Laura had not appeared for a scheduled follow-up visit, and Laura's parents told them the ulcer story. They had no comment.

Later, her mother told me that the vial of sleeping pills I had prescribed for Laura was found in her medicine cabinet, untouched. She had kept her promise not to use my pills to kill herself, and I knew she had deliberately sent me this message.

Her mother told me, with some bitterness, but mostly with sorrow and regret, that she felt professionals, such as me and others Laura had seen in the past, had nothing to offer to a person with Laura's problems and were of no help.

I thought the treatment Laura had received had helped prolong her life. But unfortunately, her illness had eventually triumphed and had killed her. I felt very sad about her death and had great regret that such a fine young person had been lost so early and so uselessly.

Her parents and her brother were devastated. Their lives were permanently damaged by Laura's suicide.

A month later, the autopsy report arrived from the medical examiner's office. Cause of death was, as expected, barbiturate overdose. The report mentioned that there were extensive abdominal scars, but that no reason could be found inside the abdomen to explain the presence of the scars. An intestinal bypass would have been apparent to the medical examiner. I became short of breath when I read this and then began to cry.

She had not lost any weight after either operation because the surgeons had done two sham operations. They had killed Laura's hope by lying to her. In my opinion, they had murdered her.

Her body had been cremated and the ashes scattered—there was no remaining physical evidence of any kind. The surgeons, who had always been haughty and irritable, had no doubt covered their tracks, either with false operative reports or possibly a claim that Laura was the placebo part of a double-blind study of bypass procedures, and that therefore they had done nothing wrong and had only followed proper experimental protocol. Or they could claim the autopsy report was incorrect, and in the absence of her body, there was no way to decide this.

I felt that if her parents and her brother learned Laura had been destroyed by the surgeons, their lives would be damaged much more than they already had been. Just as at Dr. Good's hospital some years before, there was almost no possibility of successfully accusing and bringing to justice the culprit surgeons. And there was a high probability they would bring a slander suit against whoever accused them.

This was a true ethical, existential dilemma. I was the only person in possession of all the facts. Any course of action or inaction had great potential for doing harm and almost no potential for helping. I was the only person who could choose what to do about this dreadful situation, and I could not avoid choosing.

There was no good choice. I chose to remain silent, thinking this would do the least harm. I chose to carry the burden alone.

Perhaps I made the right choice. This tragedy and my decision have haunted me for many years.

A few years later, Dr. Good was prosecuted for malpractice and abuse of patients. He was convicted and had to sign an affidavit stating the he had abused his patients by beating them with riding crops.

Chapter 4

Fun with the *Wall Street Journal*

About twenty years ago, in 1994, while leafing idly through the *Wall Street Journal*, my eye fell on a small article with a picture of a middle-aged man, Robert Monroe. The article got off to a fast start: (quoting from memory) "Leading corporations send their executives to study intuition and out-of-body experiences at an unusual institute."

The article went on to say that Robert Monroe, the man in the picture—a successful businessman, a former owner of television and radio stations, and an amateur musician—had established a center in the Blue Ridge Mountains of Virginia to study various unusual experiences. These included intuition; accelerated learning through expanded states of consciousness; out-of-body experiences (OBEs), which Monroe had been having spontaneously for the past thirty years; communication between the two brain hemispheres; voyages to the distant past and faraway planets; surgical support and other physical therapies; helping newly deceased spirits; and communication with discarnate beings. He had written three books about these matters and described pathways in other worlds, which he called the "Interstate."

I immediately acquired and read the books, marveling at the experiences he described in a calm and matter-of-fact voice. These experiences were not connected with any form of religion, although there is some mention of helpers in other dimensions. But Monroe does suggest that we consider with an open mind that we might be more than our physical bodies. I put his books on the shelf.

I had recently retired from psychiatric practice, had sold my family oil field service business, and was thinking of selling my house in the country, which was large, beautiful, old, and very time- and money-consuming to care for. I had recently separated from Bert (who was more trouble, and more exciting, than the old house). This reorganization had left me with free time and open plans for the next chapter of my life. What should I do? What would be the best way to use my next years to be productive and helpful to my fellow man? I felt that the necessary next step should be in the area of exploration of my own mental and psychological capacities.

A close friend of my cousin in Houston was to be the hostess for the Dalai Lama during his upcoming visit there. My cousin and her friend tried to arrange a private meeting for me with the Dalai Lama for me to ask his advice as to what I should do with my life, but his schedule was too full, even with these advocates trying to help me to squeeze in an appointment. Perhaps that was his answer.

"Go and work out your own salvation with diligence," the Buddha had said as his final comment before he entered Nirvana.

Two or three years later, I heard a psychiatrist speak at a meeting on the subject of transpersonal psychology. The speaker had attended some courses at the Monroe Institute, and he felt they had been interesting and helpful. I spoke to him after his lecture and then looked up the Institute on the Internet, where there was considerable information. I reread Monroe's books.

Monroe had discovered that playing tones of separate pitches in the two ears—say, 440 cycles per second in one ear and 444 cycles per second in the other ear—would cause the listener to hear a tone with four beats per second. This was not at all like hearing the two frequencies in the open air, where the peaks and valleys of the sound waves physically coincided to produce four beats a second in the air. As the tones were now sent through earphones into each ear separately and then carried by the auditory nerves to the two separate hemispheres of the brain, it must be the brain itself that was producing the four beats per second through the mechanism of communication and cooperation between the two hemispheres. Monroe called this process hemisync (hemispheric synchronization).

As Monroe changed the pitches of the tones and the speed of their movements up and down the scale, he could measure changes in the brain waves as recorded by the electroencephalogram, and these changes corresponded with various psychological states, such as deep meditation, happiness, and other conditions usually considered to be only produced by mental mechanisms. Some experienced meditators said that this procedure resulted in mental states that were similar to mental states experienced after prolonged periods of meditation.

It was obvious that any programs listened to in this hemisync procedure required good earphones with separate right and left channels

I decided to enroll for a course at the Institute. They insisted that all newcomers sign up for the introductory course called Gateway Voyage. I was eager to start, and as the airplane descended into the Charlottesville airport, I wondered what I might encounter. I hoped I might gain further insight into my mental apparatus, but ideas of an OBE were not prominent in my expectations. I was sorry that Monroe himself had died a few years earlier, but his daughter was still present and running the Institute.

A minivan was waiting to take the three students who had just arrived on the same airplane to the Institute, about ten miles out of town in beautiful rolling country in sight of the nearby Blue Ridge Mountains. The main building was an attractive long, low structure built on the side of a hill, one story in the front and two stories in the back where the hill descended. A four-story glass tower was positioned at one end, and there were various outbuildings, including a laboratory building, a giant five-foot tall crystal standing in a field, and a maze to stroll in.

The rooms had an unusual feature. My room, a single as I had requested, had a private bathroom, a small desk and desk chair, an easy chair, and a window. The bed was built into an alcove so that it had a wall at the head and foot of the bed and along one side. On the fourth side, there was a two-foot section of wall extending from the head of the bed along the open side, and the rest of that side of the bed had a sturdy brass rod with heavy blackout curtains that could be manually operated. It was like a cubicle with a curtain on one side.

Monroe Institute

There were speakers installed in the walls on either side of the pillow, pointing toward the head of the occupant. This made possible stereophonic broadcasts from a central station. There was also an outlet for stereophonic headsets. All the students could hear the same hemisync program at one time. These bed alcoves were called check units. The programs were generally lectures or interesting music.

At lunch I met my fellow students, seven women and four men, average age about forty-five. Most were from the United States, but there were students from Switzerland, South Africa, Japan, and Cyprus. None of them were weirdly dressed or otherwise odd appearing—they looked like a crowd of passengers on an airplane. There were four facilitators (trainers, guides), all cheerful and pleasant.

Some of the students and the staff reported frequent and helpful contact with Mr. Monroe, who was still present in spirit and remained active in guiding the affairs of the Institute. I did not personally have any contact with him.

We were full of anticipatory questions. "How will we know when we are getting close to an OBE?" I asked.

Susan, one of the trainers, said, "We don't want to prejudice or distort your experiences ahead of time. Just watch with an open mind. Now go to your rooms, get comfortable, and relax in your check units with the draperies pulled closed. You should be in total darkness. A one-hour exercise will be played through your earphones. Afterward, we will all gather in the common room to discuss our experiences."

We dispersed quickly, eager to get started with our new experiences. In a few minutes a lecture started coming from the speakers, explaining hemisync, with examples. Then we were told to observe our internal states while hemisync music was played.

I was a little tired and was afraid I might just go to sleep. After resting in my alcove for about ten minutes, I began to feel a very fine and enormously rapid vibration coming from inside my body. I wondered if this was a sign of something unusual about to happen. In about five minutes, I found myself sitting on my desk chair outside my check unit.

How did that happen? There was no lapse in consciousness. I had not gone to sleep, I was not asleep in the desk chair, and I did not recall getting out of bed, but there was a definite disconnect between my experience inside the check unit and my experience outside the check unit. My mental and emotional state seemed about as usual. After remaining seated on the desk chair for about sixty seconds, I looked around the darkened room but saw nothing unusual. Physically, I felt as usual. So I concluded that I was having an out-of-body experience. I wanted to try moving around, and so I slowly rose from the desk chair to a standing position. Everything seemed normal. I was curious and not afraid.

Perhaps I could go out into the hall. As I approached the door, somehow it became hazy and insubstantial, and I went through the solid physical door into the hall. Turning left, I walked along the hall about fifty or sixty feet. I noticed that I was not really walking but was gliding along the hall with my feet perhaps six or eight inches off the floor. I stopped moving my legs but continued moving forward as I wished to do. I understood that my motion was dictated by my mental state, and I had only to think I was walking to produce a facsimile of walking. I was conscious of how calm I continued to be about this experience.

If I could progress along the hall, perhaps I could also levitate, and so I wished to rise up and shortly began to rise about one foot per second. As I approached the ceiling, I wondered what was coming next. I went up through the ceiling and the roof with no obstruction, just like passing through a bit of fog. I soon emerged above the roof and continued to rise. As I became slightly uneasy and wished to stop the motion, it stopped, and I hovered very comfortably about twenty feet above the roof. Looking around, I could clearly see the immediate surroundings of the building and decided to take a small tour in the air around the perimeter of the building, perhaps twenty feet or so out from all sides of the building.

Very soon I became aware of four giant humanlike figures, each about thirty feet tall, standing at the four corners of the building.

Later I was told these were guards protecting the people inside as they entered their unusual psychic states, and I felt reassured seeing these beings, although I had not been afraid or uneasy before.

I decided to finish this experience, and so I descended gently to the front lawn and then glided through the front door of the main building and along the corridor to my room. When I reached my room, I moved into the check unit and lay down in my body.

Soon I opened my eyes, and all seemed quite usual. I got up and went back to the common room, where some of the other students had already gathered. We all described our experiences. Two of the students had OBEs, and the others had a variety of experiences. A very attractive woman, about forty years old, a doctor from a nearby town, said, "I used to have these OBEs from the time I was four years old, but after a few years, something unpleasant and frightening happened, like being raped, and so I tried not to have OBEs, and they gradually shut down. Now that I am older, I feel I can protect myself better, and so I want to do some more exploration." This sounded ominous; perhaps this OBE practice was not without dangers, but I was not afraid.

Two days later, when we were doing another exercise with hemisync, I decided to levitate less tentatively, wished to ascend, and suddenly shot up about three hundred feet before willing the ascent to stop. I was surprised that I could see (through the roof of the main building) my body lying in the check unit three hundred feet below. Somehow this great height startled me, and I wished to descend, and so within about one minute I was hovering two feet above my body. During the next thirty seconds, I reentered my body, seemed to connect with it, and the experience was over. I went out of the check unit and sat on my desk chair for a few minutes before walking out to the common room. While I described this experience, the other students listened with interest. Nobody had any comments on the mechanism of what had happened to me or on its significance.

The other students had somewhat similar experiences. Later on that week during hemisync exercises, I encountered beings whose natures were not entirely clear to me. I presumed they were discarnate entities or possibly souls of the dead. They were not ominous or threatening and did not seem interested or curious about me. Their only reaction to me was a quick and casual glance, much like what might happen when walking on a city sidewalk. They were no more ominous or threatening than the usual crowds that might be encountered on a busy city sidewalk.

After I reported to the group about my encounters with these beings, the attractive doctor spoke to me in private. She said, "My grandfather, whom I loved so much, died two years ago. I haven't had any communication from him in over a year, and I'm worried about him. When you are encountering afterlife beings, could you please keep your eye out for him? Maybe you could find him for me? His name is _____."

"Okay," I said. "I'll do my best."

During the next month, when on the other side, I broadcast his name mentally with a request to speak with him. That same day he approached me -- a medium-sized, later middle-aged-appearing man, pleasant and intelligent, just as described by my doctor friend. (The way the dead souls appear to us is a separate subject. They communicate telepathically and realize they must be recognizable when necessary.) I gave him her message. He said he was well and would try to contact her. This locating and/or reorienting of dead souls is referred to as soul retrieval. I passed on his message, which she was pleased to receive. Later she told me she was happy that her grandfather had contacted her.

This is the phenomenology of my experience. I did not understand what had happened but was inclined to accept the experience at face value (actual OBEs), as described above. There were, of course, many alternative explanations, mostly designed to explain away what had happened to me. Perhaps I had fallen asleep and had a dream, perhaps group suggestion, perhaps wishful thinking, perhaps hallucinations, self-hypnosis, psychosis, something I had eaten, etc. Maybe one or more of these items was the cause of my experiences, but I don't think so.

There had been no efforts on the part of the Institute to sell books, collect money/donations, or sign us up for ongoing programs, courses, or political agendas. But tapes and books were offered in the bookstore, as was information about future programs at MI, as it was sometimes called.

The students said good-bye to one another and departed for home. I wondered what my next step would be. All the other students I met were intelligent, pleasant, and serious. None seemed deranged, peculiar, or threatening. Since then, I have pursued similar experiences and have kept practicing, using hemisync tapes with interesting and wide-ranging results and have returned to the Monroe Institute for one further course in time exploration.

Our reality is much richer than I had ever suspected. (And that's not the half of it!)

Chapter 5

A Spring Day

Note: This is the negotiated censored version of this chapter, as agreed to with the Empress Alexandra of Russia. This chapter, along with the information contained in chapters 6 and 7, serve as background and introduction for the presentation of an important message from one of the deceased imperial Romanovs to someone in more modern times.

My friend Rick told me of this communication from the Grand Duchess Olga (1882-1960), sister of Nicholas II and daughter of the dowager Empress Maria Feodorovna (1847-1928).

It was a brilliant spring day in mid-May 1917. He was in his favorite office, which was in the family's home, the Alexander Palace, the place where he felt safest and most at ease. This is what I saw there: The room was about twenty by thirty feet with a sixteen-foot mahogany ceiling, coffered, painted green, and sparingly gilded. The office was paneled in polished maple. Simple carved floral swags surrounded niches holding Chinese porcelains. The book cases held leather-bound volumes of geography, history, and military strategy. A magnificent blue and rose Kerman carpet covered the parquet floor. Around his desk stood four straight oak chairs, and around the room were arranged lounge chairs and two black leather sofas. On the walls were many paintings of various sizes—hunting and fishing scenes, landscapes, and of course, portraits of his parents.

Mounted on a wall plaque, placed where he could see it clearly, was a brown trout. He had caught it himself many years earlier when his parents took him on a visit to the imperial fishing lodge at Langinkoski. It had been a happy time for him. Now he sometimes even imagines the trout is smiling at him. His wife, Alix, complained it was not appropriate for the office of the Czar of Russia, but he had put his foot down, for once disobeying her dictate.

Alexander Palace

On the wall opposite his desk, two large arched windows flanked a pair of French doors, which were open to a sparkling early spring scene. The air was brilliantly white, and the cold spring wind puffed across the lawn. Large lavender lilac bushes in tubs stood on either side of the French doors, sending clouds of fragrance into the office, and two pots of pink hyacinths had been placed just inside the doors, adding to the perfumed scene. Stepped stone terraces with large black-and-white checkerboard paving led down to the lawn—

youngest spring green, planted with tulips in formal patterns. It was mid-May, and he looked forward to seeing tulips in full bloom again, bravely showing their cheerful colors.

About one hundred feet from the window was the small green lake contained by three-foot-high stone retaining walls. In warm weather he occasionally permitted the children, even Alexei, to splash and play in the water. In the center of the lake was a magnificent fountain depicting sea horses and mermaids with water jets and sprays shooting up about twenty feet. In the blazing sunlight the water droplets glittered as they flew trembling and twisting through the air.

Nicholas and Alexandra

About three hundred feet from the palace a forest of birch and dark fir trees stretched across the horizon. They screened out any signs of his great capital city of St. Petersburg.

Looking at this familiar vista helped to calm him.

He seated himself at his desk—made of light Karelian birchwood inlaid with thin lines of ebony and rosewood with gold wires inlaid in a crosshatch pattern. The top was covered with pale green leather. Sturdy legs gave the desk an air of stability and practicality. He was proud of his desk, as the design was entirely his own, but it had been made, of course, by the imperial furniture makers.

Because of the recent difficulties, he had mostly cleared off the top of the desk. The only items remaining were a simple pen box, a carved nephrite ashtray on short gold legs, an enameled matchbox, a simple blue chalcedony bell-push set with a large sapphire button, and some family photographs set in jeweled frames.

A crystal vase was filled with lemon blossoms, which were brought daily to his office from the palace hothouses. He remembered dreamily a time when roomfuls of fresh flowers were sent daily from the greenhouses of the imperial estates in Crimea. The scent of the lemon blossoms mingled with the fragrance of the lilacs and the hyacinths to make a hypnotic, anesthetic perfume. He was almost in a trance from the exquisite beauty of his surroundings.

A servant brought in a cup of tea and a small glass of Tokay, silently set them on the desk, and then left the room. He glanced at the document on his desk, which he had drawn up himself. It was a grant of land to some of the farm workers at Livadia, his beloved estate in Crimea, and also a grant of one thousand acres to the foreman of his vineyards at Massandra, his great chateau and estate on the other side of Crimea. His wife and his finance minister had opposed this grant, and so he had put it off until now. He hoped it was not too late. He signed and sealed the document and set it to one side. He leaned back in his lime-green leather armchair and sighed as he contemplated his collection of fine, small Buddha figures.

He thought of other troubled monarchs. The old raven, the Dowager Empress Cixi in Peiping, had one day arranged the murder of her nephew, the Emperor Kuang Hsu, and then the next day she herself died unexpectedly, which cancelled her plans to tighten her rule over China. The Chinese emperor, poor little Pu Yi, only two years old, was left all alone on the Dragon Throne until he was forced to abdicate four years later.

The czar thought of his enemy in Japan, the hated Mutsuhito, who had died five years before, leaving his sickly son Yoshihito on the Chrysanthemum Throne, but how much longer could that one hold on? He realized the life of a monarch is not always easy or comfortable or safe.

And now in March of this year he himself had been forced to abdicate by the traitor Kerensky and some of his own army officers, who had placed him, his wife, and his five children under house arrest. "For your own protection," Kerensky said, lying with a smile.

His mother, other family members, and those who needed to see him were allowed into the palace to visit or take care of business. Neither he nor his wife or children were permitted to leave the grounds of the Alexander Palace, a few miles outside St. Petersburg, which had been their home for many years. So far, he had received the same deferential and respectful treatment as always, but he knew the situation was untenable, serious, perhaps ominous.

He thought of happier times at his beloved Livadia, his beautiful white marble palace in Crimea, sitting on the side of a great hill, looking out over the Black Sea. Opening the top-left drawer of his desk, where he kept personal items, he removed one of his favorite pieces, a gold cigarette box whose top was in the form of a map. The green fields of Crimea were shown in pave emeralds, the Black Sea was shown in pave blue sapphires, and the road to Livadia was traced out with small rubies. Livadia itself was marked by a large diamond.

His mother had designed the box herself and had commissioned Carl Fabergé to manufacture it as a surprise gift for his birthday four years ago. Nikki had been immensely moved by his mother's sweet thoughtfulness, especially since Alix's jealous unkindness to his mother had kept her at a distance for the past ten years, causing her to move her residence out of St. Petersburg to her palace in Kiev.

He hoped his mother might reach Livadia safely and that a British rescue vessel sent by her sister, Queen Alexandra of England, might be waiting to take her and the other family members to sanctuary. He slowly removed a cigarette from the case and began to smoke.

(Note: The author has seen this cigarette case, which was sold at an auction at Christie's in New York as part of a huge auction sale of Russian treasures about ten years ago, about the year 2002.)

He finished the cigarette, his cup of tea, and the glass of finest Tokay from Massandra, his own vineyard. He wistfully remembered he had five thousand bottles of this wine set aside, safe in the Livadia cellars. He rang for the servant, who cleared away the teacup and the wineglass.

The Vision Begins

Author's note: The author has sensed (or seen) these visions from long ago himself, presumably received by him telepathically.

A sudden cold west wind sent a chill into the room. The dark purple clouds moved rapidly and soon began to obscure the sun. Through breaks in the clouds, ugly burning yellow rays moved like searchlights across the ground, as if hunting for small animals to incinerate. He realized the terrible vision was starting again. The first raindrops splattered heavily on the terrace. He felt an awful premonition of disaster and tragedy.

Alix

The footman quietly announced, "Her Majesty, the czarina," and Alix briskly entered the room. She was wearing his favorite gown, a light yellow silk gown with lace at the wrists and collar, which showed off her slender figure. Her dark hair was pulled back and tied with a simple pale green ribbon, revealing her lovely face, perfect complexion, and large dark eyes. She was wearing only a few pieces of jewelry—a small diamond clip at her throat, a gold belt set with cabochon amethysts, and the unusual rose-gold and opal ring that granny Victoria had given her twenty years earlier. He found her appearance bewitching. Her expression was serious but vivacious—

he could not read her mood—no doubt she would soon enough reveal what she wanted.

"Alix, what a delightful surprise to see you. How are you?" he asked.

"Nicky dearest, I needed to see my darling husband. I wanted to feel your strength and confidence," she said, seating herself seductively close to his desk. She was obviously trying to cajole him, although she truly found his handsome face and athletic figure in his uniform quite attractive and sexually stimulating. She well knew that his exercise program, rigidly followed, had had very good results in producing a powerful physique.

Nicky: The Vision

He felt the chilling premonition sweep over him again, and the vision continued. As he continued to gaze out the doors, the clouds turned an ugly red color, like blood clots floating in the sky, and the raindrops turned to blood drops, which fell in ever heavier torrents. The lawn was soon covered with blood; the terraces were streaming with blood; and the fountains, like severed arteries, were spurting large sluggish jets of blood. The waters of the little lake had turned a dull brown, and the turgid waves threw up reddish-bronze foam as they broke against the bloody retaining walls.

Alix

Alix didn't see what her husband saw. She began to lead into her subject. "In this difficult time, Nicky, it is important that I should always be well dressed, so I can be a credit and a help to you, and our people should be reassured that all is going on in a proper manner." She was too full of pride to accept the fact that they were under house arrest; that their situation had changed.

"I have heard that Karl Fabergé recently received a large pigeon blood ruby of highest quality. Oh, yes, I know it's likely very expensive … and it's wartime. But it would make you feel better to buy it for me, and our subjects would be reassured and would be more admiring than ever. And besides, you know that red is my

81

favorite color." She gave him a frosty look as she recalled her cherished fantasy of sitting astride a writhing blood-red dragon. She felt a thrill of sexual excitement as she imagined the serpent's muscular body coiling between her legs.

Nicky: The Vision

As he looked out the doors again, a surreal scene opened before him. He saw that the lawn was no longer smooth. It was now covered with many thousands of severed human heads from Russian soldiers, mostly battered and mutilated, oozing tissues hanging in threads from the bones. Some of the heads were missing eyes, ears, or jaws. Most were dead, although a few were still alive. Some had an arm attached, and these were pulling themselves up into the lilacs. They dangled there helplessly like large savage bats, twisting around with hatred and agony until they died. Then they lost their grasp on the lilac branches and tumbled back to the ground. A few of the heads had both arms still attached, and these could raise themselves off the ground and hop. Some were hopping up the stairs, looking enraged, and were intent on coming into his office. They stared at Nicky fiercely through the glass and shouted curses. He was terrified.

He had done everything he could to save all of them, all of his people, to avert this disaster, but his plans had been too vague and had been thwarted by his ministers—by Grigori Rasputin and by Alix, who had become increasingly tyrannical and had almost been able to reduce Nicky to being her puppet.

He rang for a servant and asked that the doors be closed. The bloody rain increased, and the doors and windows were streaming with sheets of blood. More heads had reached the doors, and their faces were pressed against the glass, glaring at him.

On the other side of the room the stuffed fish began to hiss and writhe. It then tore itself loose from its plaque, fell to the floor, and began to slither toward Nicky's feet. Its mouth snapped wildly, revealing dozens of needle-sharp teeth. Nicky put his feet up on the desk to escape the monstrous fish, which then retreated under the hem of Alix's yellow silk skirt, waiting there in ambush.

The Empress Alexandra

Alix

Alix thought it quite rude of him to put his feet on his desk, and she was irritated that he looked so inattentive and preoccupied. She decided to turn up the pressure. "Well, Nicky, I see that you don't care what I think or feel. You don't want me to be happy." She then began to sniffle, a trick she knew always worked on the fool.

Actually, she was feeling rather morose. She began to think of poor sweet Brother Grigori, who had been brutally murdered five months earlier, on the very last day of 1916, by that disgusting homosexual transvestite Felix Yusupov and his band of plotters.

It had been almost impossible to kill Brother Grigori. Felix had poisoned him with an enormous amount of cyanide, then shot him six times in the chest, then clubbed him viciously, and finally tied his arms and shoved him, still living, headfirst down through the ice into the river Neva. There, trapped under the ice, he died of drowning.

The fact that Felix Yusupov was married to Nicky's niece Irina should not have shielded him from being shot—the punishment he deserved for his murder of the holy man.

Perhaps Felix at times felt bittersweet regret that Rasputin was no longer present.

Felix knew of the good side of Rasputin, who had walked hundreds of miles in Siberia to visit holy monasteries, who sometimes gave spiritually elevating sermons, and who was thought to have healing abilities. It was rumored that at times that Felix and Brother Grigori had been lovers, with Felix submissive under the erotic hypnotic control of Brother Grigori.

Nicky had more than once noticed Rasputin leering suggestively at himself, and he had felt a thrill of danger as he became aware of his desire to submit to Rasputin's control. Alix was too self-absorbed and arrogant to suspect she might be the next victim on the plotters' list or that Nicky himself was soon to be assassinated.

Rasputin

These murders were planned by patriots as an effort to save Russia and the monarchy from the tyrants before they both collapsed.

Alix and Rasputin

She knew that Brother Grigori had been not only a superhuman physical person but also a saintly spiritual being. She began to dream of a time when after prayer and spiritual discussion, he had said she needed forgiveness and that he would give her his forgiveness in private. Alix immediately suggested they go to her mauve boudoir.

Rasputin himself had witnessed Alix's ferocious tongue-lashings of her servants for small errors, or perhaps no errors at all. She did the same to her assistants, important government ministers, and her own children, and lately she had become so arrogant that she even publicly tongue-lashed the czar himself.

The Mauve Boudoir

Both Alix and Nicky often felt that their minds were falling apart, disintegrating. Only Rasputin was in control of his mind, and of theirs too.

The walls of Alix's mauve boudoir were covered with icons of various saints and other religious figures. They all had grim expressions, perhaps because of the many nasty and dissolute scenes that they had witnessed. They wished to turn their heads away. They wished to recover custody of their eyes but were unable to do so.

Brother Grigori said sternly, "Kneel down and bow your head. We are all sinners and must pray to God and to all the saints for forgiveness. Because you are the Empress of Russia, you are an especially guilty sinner." Brother Grigori had in mind much more thorough and forceful ways for her to expiate her sins than some mild prayers.

"I will do as you say, Holy Father," she murmured meekly as she knelt at his feet. But that was some time ago, and now Brother Grigori was dead, and she didn't have anyone to grant her forgiveness or spiritual guidance, and poor Baby had no one to cure his attacks of bleeding and pain. Still in a daze of memory, she gradually remembered she was the Empress of Russia, shut down her fantasy and slowly regained her composure.

She closed up the recollection and returned to the present.

Nicky

The horrors continued. He saw the heads of his four daughters lying beside his desk. All were battered and bleeding, their hair matted with clotted blood. Both of Olga's eyes had been shot out. Maria was missing an ear, and the wound was gushing blood. She was still alive, looking around in terror. When she saw him, he could read her pleading as they looked into each other's eyes. He turned his eyes away like a coward.

Tatiana's head and face were deeply lacerated. Her teeth were visible through the holes where parts of her face had been torn away. Anna had been shot in the face and had a gaping wound where her nose and mouth had been. She had been holding her little spaniel, Jimmy, as she was being shot to death.

Jimmy had been slightly wounded but was still alive and struggling to escape. Suddenly, Baby's head also appeared, terribly crushed and missing his jaw, blood trickling from his ears. Baby's gentle pet spaniel, Joy, landed with a thud on the pile, screaming with pain from a crushed back until he expired. Alexei's body was missing both arms. This vision broke Nicky's heart. He was breathless with sorrow.

Royal family

Then Alix's head joined the heads of their five children. Her severed head was intact, and her eyes were flashing with anger, her mouth screaming imprecations. Suddenly, a bayonet pierced her skull, entering just above her right eye and exiting below her left jaw. Her blood splattered the vicinity. The crunching noise made by the bayonet was loud enough to drown out her screaming. With a look of surprise and scorn, and with a final curse, the empress closed her eyes in death.

Then he saw his own head appear, the back of his skull blown off by bullets, the wound oozing blood and brain tissue. Some last tears were still flowing from his wide-open eyes, which were staring at a final emptiness. This was a terrible sight.

The harsh, strident voice of the czarina recalled Nicky brutally to the present. "Get the ruby for me now, you weak worm," she commanded.

Nicky and Alix

Now they were both firmly in current reality. He was tired of the tedious conversation with Alix. She already had so many rubies she could make a necklace long enough to reach down to hell. Nicky now saw her as intolerably greedy, coarse, revolting. He remembered when they first met—when Alix was a kind young princess, innocent and loving. What had happened to her? How could she have turned into this monstrous, hardened shrew? Was it his fault? Had he not shown her enough love? Of course, he knew that once Brother Grigori had come on the scene to help Baby, Alix soon slid down to become a cruel, dissipated woman of Babylonian decadence, almost as if she were trying to be evil—or trying to be like Rasputin, or worthy to be Rasputin's consort.

He knew Rasputin owned Alix, and Alix ruled the czar.

He used his telephone to call Fabergé. "Please bring your new large ruby to us tomorrow afternoon, as Her Majesty is interested to inspect and possibly acquire the stone." When Alix saw that she had achieved her goal, she abruptly said she had a headache and stood up to leave.

He said, "Good-bye, dear. I'll see you for dinner around eight o'clock. Just the family tonight."

Growing increasingly angry, as she sometimes did when an important wish had been granted, Alix rushed out without making a reply, before she lost her temper at her sissy husband, who was certainly inferior to the strong, miraculous, and ever-forgiving Brother Grigori. She hoped Nicky could soon be removed from her life. As she exited, Nicky thought he heard her utter a curse. He wished he could think of a way to rid himself of this termagant. Both were soon to have their wishes granted.

Alexei and Joy

Alexei and Joy

All Is Well

The trout had stopped snapping and had calmed itself; it wriggled back up the wall, installed itself on its plaque, and resumed smiling. Nicky walked to the French doors and slowly opened them. The bloody rain had stopped, but the nauseating stench of the

91

clotting blood filled all the rooms. The clouds had parted to reveal a terrifying roaring and whirling emerald-green sun, which sent huge glittering black lightning bolts outward in all directions. The severed heads had vanished, the blood was fading from the fields and terraces, and the fountains were again jetting crystalline water, perhaps still slightly pink. The waters of the lake were again green. The sun slowly turned white, the air brightened, and the scene was once again a lovely spring day. But occasionally screams and curses were heard coming down from the clouds.

Epilogue

Three months later, in August 1917, the imperial family, accompanied by their physician, Dr. Eugene Botkin; several attendants; and their two little pet dogs, Jimmy and Joy, were taken from the Alexander Palace to Tobolsk in Siberia, where they were imprisoned.

Eight months after that, in April and May 1918, they were all transferred to Ekaterinburg in the Ural Mountains, where they were imprisoned in the Ipatiev House, known as The House of Special Purpose.

In the basement of that house, in the early morning hours of July 17, 1918, by order of Vladimir Lenin himself, the entire imperial family was shot to death, along with their doctor, three other attendants, and their little pet dog Joy.

On the order of Boris Yeltsin, the house was demolished in 1977 so as not to become a memorial to the murdered imperial family.

Within two more days, in various locations, fourteen other members of the Romanov family, including the saintly Ella, were murdered, most dying gruesome deaths. Within six more months, five additional family members were executed in St. Petersburg. Ella, as a holy saint, was buried in Jerusalem on the Mount of Olives.

The czar's aunt, the Grand Duchess Maria Pavlovna of Mecklenburg, who was married to his uncle, the Grand Duke Vladimir, a senior member of the Romanov family, was the last family member to leave Russia. She survived for only a short while in exile, considering herself to be the last Empress of Russia because of her marriage to Grand Duke Vladimir.

Millions of people were to die in the First World War and in the Holocaust, both of which at least partly developed from the unhindered ascent of Lenin and Joseph Stalin and the instability of Russia following the death of the imperial family. The royal family seemed to some like parasites or demons or mere empty figureheads at the time, but their actual function was to preserve the structure of Russia. Many people were heartbroken or otherwise crushed as a result of the family's disappearance.

*Author's Note

On a day in May a few years ago, while I was visiting St. Petersburg, Russia, I had the opportunity to visit the Alexander Palace at Tsarskoe Selo, home to the imperial Romanov family, and where they spent their final few years before they were sent into captivity and then on to be murdered.

The palace has been restored to its appearance before the revolution. We drove up to the front entrance. There was only one other car parked there. Perhaps the Alexander Palace is not visited often.

Looking at the front of the palace, the wing on the left housed the apartments of the imperial family. The wing on the right contained the apartment of the beloved Dowager Empress Maria Alexandrovna, the last czar's mother. The palace is surrounded by gardens, fountains, open fields, and beautiful old trees.

We entered the front door and went through an entrance hall and proceeded toward the back of the building. We then continued left into a large and imposing anteroom with polished marble floors, large windows, and a sparkling crystal chandelier. Pristine stucco and marble were everywhere, and at one end a couple of chests sat along a wall. The only other piece of furniture was an elaborately carved concert grand Bechstein piano, with its bench, standing in the middle of the room. The Empress Alexandra Feodorovna was a fine pianist, and this was her piano. Passing by, I touched the keyboard and played a few notes. This produced a faraway sound, somewhat out of tune. There was a very sad aura surrounding this instrument. The imperial family would have enjoyed performances by leading pianists of the time, such as Franz Liszt, Anton Rubinstein, Sergei Rachmaninoff, and Sergei Bortkiewicz.

We progressed on into the imperial apartment and entered large, contiguous, mostly empty rooms with a fine view over the palace park and fountain. There was a haunted, troubled atmosphere here.

As we paused to look at the long-empty rooms, the air darkened slightly, and a tall figure in an old-fashioned military uniform and a long overcoat walked toward us and saluted. Extremely polite and courtly, he spoke in a low and serious voice, observing us with a hawk-like gaze.

"I have been sent as an emissary from her Imperial Majesty, the Czarina Alexandra Feodorovna. She is aware of your written account of meetings between her Majesty and Brother Grigori Rasputin."

Astounded, I was only able to murmur, "Yes, that is so."

"She is highly displeased with your account of the meetings. Although she does not dispute the accuracy of your description, she does not believe that wide public knowledge of these meetings would produce anything other than an injurious influence on the reputations of herself, the czar, Brother Grigori, and yourself. Therefore, she requests and commands that you withdraw this material from your planned publication, and she thanks you in advance for your acquiescence to her suggestion."

I was flabbergasted that the empress would send me a message like this. Apparently her reputation as an imperious and controlling person was deserved, and her ability in this regard has survived her death almost one hundred years ago. I was at a loss as how to answer. I could feel her reaching out from the grave and clutching at my shoulder.

My description of the meetings between Her Majesty and Brother Grigori was lively, factual, somewhat lurid, and also comical, and I thought of it as one of the high points of my narrative. It has been completely written and typed, but not published, and has been put away in my records for safekeeping.

However, apparently the account was offensive to Alexandra. I did not think that the omission of this material would have an important effect on my memoir. So, reluctantly I agreed that this material could be suppressed and asked the messenger to inform Her Majesty that I agreed to her request. The account will be made available to persons with a legitimate interest in this matter fifty years after the publication of this book.

*****

This has been a truly unexpected and unusual episode, but think I should report the events just as they occurred.

A few days later, while visiting the Hermitage, the Winter Palace, as I walked through the rooms they seemed absolutely familiar, just as when you enter your own home and it seems familiar. This was especially true of the throne room, one of the large reception rooms, and the private apartments of the imperial family. The source of this feeling of familiarity is not known to me, but it was very striking at that time.

Rick and guide, Winter Palace, St. Petersburg)

Author and Rick at Yusupov Palace)

Prince Felix Yusupov and his wife, the Princess Irina

Author and Rick at Livadia Palace, Crimea

Beach at Yalta

Author and Rick at Livadia Palace, Crimea

Russian Orthodox Church near Livadia Palace, Crimea

Mariyinsky Palace, Kiev, home of the Dowager Empress Maria Feodorovna

Swallow's Nest, another Romanov palace in Crimea

Chapter 6

At the Train Station

The needless deaths and brutal slaughter of twenty-five million people might have been averted if the meeting had ended differently.

The meeting, which affected the course of history during most of the twentieth century, took place on March 17, 1917, at Mogilev, a small city and rail junction five hundred miles south of St. Petersburg. Only two persons were present at the meeting, both of the highest rank. Several other important people were close by, just outside the meeting room, but they were neither invited nor permitted to enter. The two persons attending the meeting never revealed what was said or even what the topics of discussion were.

The two persons were Maria Feodorovna, Dowager Empress of Russia, and her son, Nicholas II, the last Czar of Russia.

The Empress Marie had been born in 1847 in Denmark. She was born the Princess Dagmar, daughter of King Christian IX and Queen Louise of Denmark. She had been cared for as befits a royal princess and grew up to be beautiful, gracious, and kind. Educated and intelligent, she had common sense and an extremely strong sense of duty, probity, and responsibility. Princess Dagmar, who was called Minnie in the family, was closely related to many of the royal persons of Europe. Her sister Alexandra married King Edward VII of England and so became Queen of England. Her brother became King George I of Greece.

She had been betrothed to the Czarevich Nicholas, called Nixa, oldest son of Czar Alexander II of Russia. Nicholas was tall and handsome, lively, charming, and intelligent. The young couple was very much in love. The princess was warmly welcomed into the Russian imperial family. The marriage plans had been made, and the union would have important benefits for both Denmark and Russia, and also for the two ruling families.

The Empress Maria Feodorovna

However, Nixa had a serious lung ailment, became increasingly ill, and died of tubercular meningitis on April 24, 1865, a few months before the wedding was scheduled to take place. Dagmar, now only age eighteen, was heartbroken.

The Romanovs had been enchanted by Dagmar. A few months after Nixa's death, they began to mention her possible marriage to their second son, Alexander, who was now the heir to the throne. Alexander (called Sascha) was very tall and enormously strong, with a heavy build and a complete lack of grace.

He was placid, generous, and unsociable. He had sound common sense and a rigid code of morality. Dagmar expressed interest, and after a few months, they were engaged. Dagmar converted to the Russian Orthodox faith, receiving the name Maria Feodorovna (often called Marie in the family), and their marriage took place on November 9, 1866. After his father died, Sascha inherited the throne and was crowned Alexander III, and his new tsaritza was, of course, Maria Feodorovna (a.k.a. Princess Dagmar, Minnie, Maria and Marie).

Alexander loved Dagmar from the start, but Dagmar only slowly moved from fondness and respect to love. They had a mostly happy union, sometimes clouded by Sascha's heavy drinking. There were six children: Nicholas II (1868–1918), Grand Duke Alexander (1869–1870), Grand Duke George (1871–1899), Grand Duchess Ksenia (1875–1960), Grand Duke Michael (1878–1918), and Grand Duchess Olga (1882–1960).

The new empress was conscientious in fulfilling all her imperial responsibilities, was a loving wife, a fond and attentive mother, and sociable and charming. Sascha often discussed affairs of state with her. As years went by, the empress not only became very popular with the Romanovs, the other aristocrats, and the military, but also with the Russian people. She was a shrewd and thoughtful observer and developed astute and sophisticated judgment about both personal and governmental matters. She also learned Russian, which many of those marrying into the imperial family were not willing to do.

In January 1894, Sascha entered a period of failing health and was diagnosed with nephritis, a serious kidney disorder. Further alcohol was forbidden, but he had a special pair of boots made with a secret compartment to hold a flask, so he could escape the watchful eye of the empress as he continued to indulge. After many months of decline, he died on November 1, 1894, at the age of forty-nine. The Empress Marie was then forty-seven and was once again heartbroken. After a period of grieving, she resumed her duties, now as the dowager empress, and was much respected in her family and by the Russian government for her wisdom and good advice. She remained in Russia for the next twenty-five years, until 1919, and she lived through the horrors of the revolution of 1917.

Even though she had lived an exemplary life in Russia for fifty-three years, she was barely able to escape the murderous Bolsheviks to seek refuge in England and Denmark, dying in 1928.

Marie's son Nicholas, age twenty-six at the time of his father's death, had been brought up as was customary for the heir to the Russian throne. However, his father never discussed affairs of government with Nicholas or tried to prepare him in any way for his future position as Czar of Russia. Alexander seldom lost a chance to criticize and ridicule his son for the smallest mistake or infraction. His father destroyed his self-confidence. Perhaps he perceived Nicholas as a weak person, and this might have stimulated his sadism.

Nicholas had not been interested in his schoolwork but received adequate education, with the customary emphasis on military matters. In his younger life, he was a playboy, as was usual with the Russian grand dukes. Shorter than the other Romanov males, he tried to compensate by building a powerful physique through exercise. He was shy, handsome, self-effacing, passive, and indecisive. He was very attached to and much influenced by his mother.

When he came of age to marry, he was engaged to the Princess Alix von Hesse und bei Rhein (called Alicky in the family), an extremely beautiful, haughty woman with an ice-cold personality. She was shy, unkind, and meddling and had no apparent interest in people, in Russia, or in government. In spite of living in Russia for many years, she never learned to speak or read Russian. However, she and Nicholas professed love for one another.

*****

For many months the wedding had been scheduled to take place on November 26, 1894. This turned out to be just twenty-five days after the death of Alexander III, the previous czar. Many thought this haste was quite improper and concluded that Alix was more interested in her position as tsarevna (crown princess) than she was in propriety. And they were right, as she would automatically become Czarina of Russia on the occasion of her husband's coronation as Czar Nicholas II.

At the time of her conversion to the Russian Orthodox Church, she took the name Alexandra Feodorovna. The wedding took place on schedule, even though the timing offended many, being too close to the death of the previous czar. She was off to a very bad start as future Empress of Russia. Her reputation never improved.

The coronation took place on May 26, 1896. On May 30, a coronation ball was scheduled to take place. That was also the day for the traditional coronation festivities for the peasants, with free food and beer for everyone. The party was held in a meadow just south of St. Petersburg; 500,000 peasants had gathered in honor of the new monarchs. There was a stampede over the food supply, and 1,389 peasants were trampled to death, and 1,300 were injured. Probably the true number was greater. Nicholas and Alexandra were advised not to attend the coronation ball that evening out of respect for the dead but decided to go anyway, helping to establish their reputation as heartless and selfish. Afterward, many Russians thought of Alix as the Princess of Death.

Dowager Empress Marie was the only member of the royal family to visit the injured in the hospitals.

Alexandra was hostile and unkind to her mother-in-law, Marie. Perhaps she disliked her husband's attachment to his mother. Certainly she resented the fact that the dowager empress, as a matter of protocol, ranked higher at the Russian court than she did. Alexandra's hostility was so extreme that Marie eventually moved away from her home in St. Petersburg and took up permanent residence at her palace in Kiev.

Nicholas was not equipped, nor did he have the temperament to be a proper monarch. The imperial couple had five children, Olga (born 1895), Tatiana (born 1897), Maria (born 1899), Anastasia (born 1901), and Alexei (born 1904), the czarevich.

Nicholas's reign was marked by deteriorating political stability, several abortive attempts at revolution, and finally culminated and ended in the Russian Revolution of 1917, which toppled the three hundred-year-old Romanov dynasty. Nicholas, although personally shy and insecure, was a total autocrat, resolutely opposed to democracy. In spite of this, he was viewed as extremely dependent on his wife and was viewed as henpecked, which was a correct assessment. He cared nothing for the approval or support of the people. Most of the large family of Romanovs shared this outlook.

In 1914 the First World War began. The poorly equipped and poorly supplied Russian army at first was successful but soon began to waver and disintegrate. At the urging of his wife, Nicholas, totally unfit to be the commander in chief, took over the control of the army in 1915, and was often away at the front. He left control of the government in the hands of the Czarina Alexandra and the depraved monk Grigori Rasputin. They ruled by favoritism, corruption, irritation, whim, and erratic emotional tantrums. Acting together, these two rapidly ruined the Russian government, disorganizing its structure and dismissing and disabling most of the senior officials. Half of the senior officials were suddenly dismissed without cause. This weakened any chances for the survival of the monarchy.

Three million Russian soldiers died in the war.

The Dowager Empress Marie, many of the other Romanovs, and also officials of the government tried to warn Nicholas of the urgent necessity of taking the government out of the hands of the czarina, who had become widely hated and was rumored to be a German spy, as well as the necessity of banishing Rasputin from further meddling in the government. The czar refused to do either, as by then he was totally dominated by Alexandra. He did not forgive anyone who tried to warn him against Alexandra and/or Rasputin.

Alexandra was, in turn, dominated by Rasputin, who had the mysterious ability to control and ease the pain and bleeding of Czarevitch Alexei's episodes of severe hemophilia. The heir to the throne should not be seen to be severely ill, so Alexei's affliction had been kept secret from all but the immediate family and his doctors.

Rasputin used his mysterious healing abilities to make himself indispensable to the imperial family, and perhaps he established some degree of hypnotic control over the czarina. This was a situation in which someone who was notoriously depraved and corrupt also had undisputed miraculous healing powers. It was widely rumored that Rasputin and the Empress Alexandra had become lovers. This rumor was extremely offensive to most Russians, but was widely believed.

Rasputin was murdered on New Year's Day 1917 by a group of patriotic conspirators led by Prince Felix Yusupov, husband of Princess Irina, the Empress Marie's granddaughter, who was also the czar's niece. Prince Felix and Rasputin had been sexually intimate on several previous occasions, a fact that is not generally known.

Following Rasputin's death, the precarious situation in Russia did not improve. By then, the political and economic situation in Russia had so deteriorated that nothing could stop the rushing force of the revolution. The war effort had also become a disastrous failure. Conditions spiraled downward.

Nicholas was worried by accounts of revolutionary riots in the capital, which had started on March 8, and was also concerned for his family. All the children, who were staying in the Alexander Palace outside St. Petersburg, were ill with measles. On March 15, 1917, the czar decided to return from the front to St. Petersburg. On the way back to St. Petersburg, the imperial train was blockaded. Much to his surprise, his own generals came aboard and demanded his resignation. After much discussion, he signed the abdication decree that day. His train then went on to Mogilev, where he waited for further developments.

His mother, the dowager empress, had been at her palace, the Mariyinsky Palace in Kiev. Hearing that Nicholas was in Mogilev, she ordered her train to proceed there, arriving on March 17. She was accompanied by her daughter, the Grand Duchess Olga Alexandrovna, Nikki's sister. Both trains waited side by side at the station, across the snow-covered platform from each other. It was a sad reunion.

Nicholas joined his mother in her coach. They were alone for two hours. They never revealed what was said or even the subjects of the conversation. At the end of the two hours, various persons waiting outside were invited into the czarina's railway coach.

The Grand Duke Alexander (called Sandro), Nicholas's brother-in-law and Marie's son-in-law married to the Grand Duchess Ksenia, reported that he found Marie sobbing aloud, all trace of her habitual self-control gone. Nicholas stood motionless, looking at his feet and smoking; the czar was calm but pale.

On March 21 Marie and Nicholas had lunch together in her train. A deputation arrived to escort the czar to begin his house arrest. He covered his mother's face with kisses and then strode across the platform with the few members of his suite permitted to accompany him home.

"As his train slowly pulled away, Marie could see him framed in the window, waving, with an expression of infinite sadness. Her eyes overflowing with tears, she made the sign of the Cross as his train slowly disappeared. Mother and son were never to meet again in their lifetimes." (Hall, Coryne. *Little Mother of Russia*. Holmes & Meier: New York/London, 1999, pp. 282–3.)

Prince Felix Yusupov was also present. He gave a separate, corroborating account of the same events of March 17: "At the station, Nicolas II remained alone with his mother in her private train for two hours. Their conversation was not divulged. When my father-in-law (the Grand Duke Alexander—Sandro) was invited to join them, the Empress was weeping bitterly. The Czar stood motionless and silent, smoking. Three days later the Emperor left for Tsarskoe-Selo where he was to be interned with his family in the Alexander Palace. His train was standing side by side with that of the dowager empress, who stood weeping at the window of her carriage. She made the sign of the cross and a gesture of benediction. As the train moved out, the Czar waved good-by. This was the last time he was to see his mother." (Prince Felix Yusupov, *Lost Splendor*. G.P. Putnam's Sons: New York, 1953, pp. 274–5.)

Five months later, in August 1917, the czar, the czarina, and the children were all evacuated, taken as prisoners from the Alexander Palace in St. Petersburg to Tobolsk in Siberia. Eight months after that they were moved from Tobolsk to Ekaterinburg in the Urals, where they were imprisoned in the Ipatiev House, also called the House of Special Purpose.

In the basement of this house on July 17, 1918, the entire imperial family, along with their doctor and their attendants and one of the little pet dogs, Joy, were murdered. Their bodies were dumped in a remote and hidden pit in the Siberian forest.

August 1, 1917: Imperial family removed from the Alexander Palace in St. Petersburg and taken to Tobolsk in Siberia.
April 27, 1918: Nicholas, Alexandra, and their daughter the Grand Duchess Maria were moved to Ekaterinburg in the Urals.

(Alexei was ill, and he, Olga, Tatiana, and Anastasia remained in Tobolsk.)

May 23, 1918: Alexei and his three sisters were removed to Ekaterinburg.

July 17, 1918: The entire imperial family was murdered by order of Lenin.

July 25, 1918: Ekaterinburg was liberated by Czech and White Russian armies. The imperial family could not be located.

The Ipatiev house was destroyed on orders of Boris Yeltsin in 1977, so as to eliminate any traces of the imperial family's stay.

There was one survivor of the massacre. In the murder room, Anastasia had held her beloved spaniel, Jimmy, in her arms as she was shot and killed. Jimmy was wounded, but was still alive when the shooting stopped. The murderers didn't bother to finish him off. He was able to drag himself out of that room, up the stairs, and finally escaped out of the house and onto the street. A kind passerby saw the little dog and recognized who he was.

She took him home and nursed him back to health, and he lived with her for a while, after which he was taken by an English diplomat to England, where he lived with the royal family at Windsor Castle for the next three years until he died of natural causes. He is buried under a lilac bush on the grounds of Windsor Castle, and his grave is marked by a small plaque.

Not long after the murders, a young woman was found in a canal trying to commit suicide. For a long time, she was mute, but eventually the claim was made that she was the Grand Duchess Anastasia, who had by great luck escaped the massacre. I had a friend who met this woman, Anna Anderson, several times and had talked with her. He said that, of course, he could not prove that she was the Grand Duchess Anastasia, but she was very convincing in her regal but kindly bearing. He was of the impression that she was really who she claimed to be—the Grand Duchess Anastasia, proper claimant to the throne of Russia. She was interviewed on the television numerous times and made a dignified and regal appearance.

I saw two of her television interviews, and she was quite impressive and attractive. Years later, it was proved by DNA, in cooperation with several Romanov relatives, as well as with Prince Philip of England, that she was not related to the Romanovs.

Hers was a romantic story, but no more than that.

Within two days of the executions, in various locations, fourteen other members of the Romanov family, including the saintly Grand Duchess Ella, were brutally murdered.

Six months later, another five members of the family, including Grand Duke Paul, the family patriarch, were shot to death in a prison in St. Petersburg. Other family members only reached safety when they escaped from Russia, fleeing their homeland with nothing more than they could carry. The Grand Duke Kirill Vladimirovich assumed the title of czar, but this was not recognized by other members of the Romanov family. His widow, the Grand Duchess Maria Pavlovna of Mecklenburg, (unreasonably) considered herself to be the last Empress of Russia.

Bodies of five members of the imperial family, supposedly lost, remained in the Siberian pit for more than seventy years. Then they were "found," exhumed, and eventually given a magnificent funeral. Held in St. Petersburg on July 17, 1998, the eightieth anniversary of the murders, the funeral was attended by many dignitaries and senior members of the Romanov family who were allowed to enter Russia for the first time since the Revolution of 1917. There was considerable contention within the family over matters of rank-- also within the Russian government over the church's decision to declare Nicholas a saint. Due to the religious and family controversies, the only member of European royalty to attend the funeral was Prince Michael of Kent, a distant cousin.

The bones of the murdered Romanovs, in five small coffins, were interred in the Fortress of St. Peter and St. Paul in St. Petersburg, resting place of all the other deceased imperial Romanovs. Unfortunately, the bodies of two of the imperial children, the Grand Duchess Marie and the Czarevitch Alexei, were not found until some years later, at which time they were also interred, remaining next to the tombs of their parents.

Grand Duchess Elizabeth of Russia, "Ella"

At the time of the revolution in 1917, the dowager empress managed to escape to Crimea, along with several other family members. Livadia, the magnificent white marble summer palace, as well as several imperial villas, including the estate of Massandra, were located in Crimea. It took a while for the revolution to reach Crimea, but eventually conditions deteriorated there, and it became very dangerous for the royal group. The First World War was still in progress. Numerous royal relatives, including the British, Romanian,

113

Greek, Danish, and Swedish monarchs were most concerned and did all in their power to try to help the empress and the others trapped in Crimea. The royal Russian group repeatedly rejected offers of help from the German Kaiser. Marie refused to leave Russia until the situation was extreme. In a harrowing last-minute rescue from the beach on April 11, 1919, the group was evacuated from Crimea aboard the British naval ship the battleship HMS *Marlborough* and taken to Malta, leaving many chests of silver, gold, and jewels abandoned on the beach in their haste to escape. The ship had been sent to the rescue by King George V of England, whose mother, Queen Alexandra of England, was the sister of the Empress Marie of Russia.

At the time she began her exile, Marie was seventy-two, and she had lost almost everything she held dear. She went to live in England and then on to Denmark, her childhood home. She lived a somewhat secluded life, greatly respected but very sad. The much-beloved Empress died quietly on October 13, 1928, age eighty-one. Her funeral, held in the St. Alexander Nevsky Church in Copenhagen, was attended by many members of the Romanov family, other Russian exiles, the King and Queen of Denmark, the Duke of York, and other European royals and politicians. An estimated one hundred thousand people lined the streets leading from the church to the railway station, where a train took the group twenty miles to the twelfth-century Roskilde Cathedral, burial place of the Danish royal family.

In the absence of Nicholas, or of any other suitable Romanov to serve as czar, the symbols and framework of the old authority and stability had disappeared. This led to an ongoing chaos in the Russian government and the eventual ascendancy of Lenin and then Stalin with their millions of murdered victims. Germany was no longer constrained by its traditional enemy, Russia, and this eventually led to the Holocaust and the outbreak of the Second World War with the loss of many more millions. The survival of the Russian Czar may well have deflected all this tragedy, perhaps even stopped it entirely.

After lengthy negotiations between the governments of Denmark and Russia and the Romanov family, plans were made for the return of Marie's body to Russia, as she had always wished. In September 2006 her coffin was removed from the Roskilde Cathedral outside Copenhagen and taken in a somber and lengthy procession, led by the Queen of Denmark and accompanied by many royals and other dignitaries to the harbor in Copenhagen, put aboard a Danish ship draped with imperial flags, and taken to Peterhof Palace near St. Petersburg, where she would lie in state.

A magnificent funeral wound solemnly through the streets of St. Petersburg, the last imperial Romanov funeral that could ever be held.

Marie was then reinterred with great ceremony next to her husband, Nicholas II, in St. Peter and St. Paul Cathedral, as it was her wish to be buried there.

HMS Marlborough

A few years earlier, in 1989, a somewhat similar funeral had occurred, at the time of the death of the Empress Zita of Bourbon-Parma, last Hapsburg Empress of the Austro-Hungarian Empire. Huge crowds were in attendance.

My friend, Ambassador Tine Ferringa of the Netherlands, was present and told me the ceremonies were immensely solemn and moving.

Chapter 7

Meeting a New Friend

In 1999, Liz, one of my Tokyo friends, told me that a new member of Alcoholics Anonymous had recently arrived in Tokyo, a young American man from Chicago who had told her he was gay, knew nobody in Tokyo, and felt lonely. She asked me if I would meet him and talk with him. And so, shortly after that, Rick and I met for lunch. I found him very pleasant, intelligent, and attractive, but also somehow elusive, and we really didn't connect.

Steve rejoined his former firm and began his new job in the London office in 2000. I continued my back-and-forth routine—one month in London and the next month in New York. In 2002 Steve arranged for a transfer back to Tokyo, and I again tagged along to Tokyo with my usual back-and-forth schedule.

I contacted Rick and invited him to have lunch with me. We began to have lunch every Thursday before the AA meeting. Our first Thursday lunch was on October 16. We told each other something of our histories—personal, drinking, and sexual—and found we shared many past experiences. Rick told me that since age six he had been fascinated by Dowager Empress Marie and the final years of the Romanov dynasty.

He knew an impressive amount of detail about this subject. He asked me if I had seen a photograph of the Czarina Alexandra's mauve boudoir, which I had not. In turn, I told him of my interest in Czar Nicholas II and in the extermination of the imperial family in 1918 and my thoughts about the subject.

Rick and author, Tokyo, Japan

The following Thursday, Rick brought along his partner, Glenn, who was living in Wellington, New Zealand, but was visiting Tokyo for his holiday. We had a very pleasant meeting. Glenn, an intelligent, good-looking, intense man about Rick's age, told me he was working on a novel. I asked him if he would read something I had recently written and make comments and suggestions, as I had just started writing and would appreciate some advice. He agreed, and the next week I sent him a piece about Czar Nicholas in his last days in St. Petersburg. He returned this in about three weeks with extensive and helpful comments. He obviously had read my piece carefully and thoughtfully. I was grateful for this help.

Rick and I talked about books we were reading, and I told him about Prince Felix Yusupov's memoirs, *Lost Splendor*. A few days later, I sent him my copy, which he read with interest and enthusiasm. It was widely thought by their contemporaries that perhaps Prince Felix and Rasputin had been sexually involved.

I had been curious when reading the book as to what had happened at the Mogilev train station on March 17, 1917.

As Rick often seemed to have extensive knowledge of the private activities of the imperial family, I asked him what he thought might have taken place during the private meeting between the dowager empress and the czar in her railway car.

Two days later, he sent me the following reply via e-mail:

Insight into the Passage:

The Dowager Empress Marie is utterly heartbroken and angry with him. She could not believe that Nicky has allowed this to happen and that his wife Alix has played a huge role in his demise. On the one hand she wants him and the children to go to England to be with her sister's family (i.e., Queen Alexandra of England, married to the King of England)—but on the other hand she knows he cannot leave his country—this is the heartbreak. Oh, the frustration she feels at him for not having been stronger, like his father, as well as for not listening to her. All of this could have been avoided. Nicky is completely stoic—emotionless, dry, surrendering to a destiny that he believes will make his life simpler and calmer—no frustrations.

His mother knows better. She sees what is happening—she has always been politically astute. He should leave with her now and send for the family later—the guards on the train are still friendly to them, and this will be his one last chance. She told him this. It was below her dignity and his. He simply looked away when she uttered the words, and the moment they left her mouth she regretted having said them. It was over then, their meeting and their communication.

At first he had surrendered to her, grateful to be with her during this terrible time, scarcely believing it was happening. They talked of the situation, Alix, the children, his health and safety, which loyal servants were with him. Then her anger flew at him—why did he have to do this—to listen to Alix and the others who were shoving the last dagger in his back? He agreed to some extent with her—it was the first time he allowed himself to believe her and the rumors he

119

knew were circulating about the situation. He released for one moment into her arms and buried his head on her shoulder. It was then that her motherly instinct took over, and she begged him to leave with her for England. Marie didn't know where these words came from or how they left her body; they simply flew out before she could pull them back in.

He released his grip on her and pulled away. This was all too unbelievable. No, Alix was right, his mother was not in touch with what was going on. He needed to be back with Alix as quickly as possible. He left his mother then. The small door of recognition, love, and truth closed as quickly as it had opened. He could never leave Russia—he never would. In the face of everything he had done wrong—he would never leave his country. It would be his only heroic act in life. His mother saw that. She regretted that she had tried to take that away from him. She knew this was the only way her son could be a leader and respected in his own eyes. He had to go with the guards, and this broke her heart in so many places. Her dreams, her life, her world were crashing down around her. She had failed even herself by groveling for him to leave with her. By the time the others started to come in, mother and son had already said good-bye.

(December 18, 2003: Rick's reply to my e-mail of December 16, 2003)

As I read what Rick had written, a brilliantly glittering world seemed to come gliding forward out of the fog—engulfing, desperate, hopeless, and utterly familiar. I wondered how Rick knew all this, and I was certain that the account in his letter was absolutely accurate.

A few days later, I asked him, "Rick, how did you find out the information about what went on in the private meeting between Marie and Nicki in Marie's railroad car?"

"This is what I saw when I thought about the event," he said.

I replied, "But neither one of them ever revealed to anyone what had been discussed."

His answer was stunning. Rick looked at me for a moment and then said, "She told Olga, who passed the information on to me." (Marie's daughter, the Grand Duchess Olga, who had been accompanying her mother on this trip to Mogilev.) This information was given to Rick by Olga in that region where multiple universes, multiple worlds, and multiple beings all exist simultaneously and in the same place; not here, not there, not yet, and where past, present, and future together form the merest suggestion of the base of that reality.

In that location excursions and voyages of truly incredible length and duration, almost infinite (to our understanding), could at the same time be started and completed within a few seconds by taking account of, going around or through the folds of spatial reality. This velocity of travel was faster than the speed of sound, faster than the speed of light, as fast as the speed of thought, of imagination, finishing the excursion with the speed of imaginary presentation.

I do not know, even in the vaguest outline, what the speed of imaginary presentation might mean, this is what I heard described. Perhaps more will be revealed in the future. In what I hope will be the not too distant future we may all be able to enter that region at will to begin trips of tremendous length and duration through space and time, again almost infinite, which at the same time will take very little or no time or effort to complete. Perhaps teachers and guides, great beings of light, will teach us how to travel this way so that we may escape our present predicament.

Immensely powerful and destructive forces will attempt to annihilate our universe and destroy time, leaving behind only faint orphan memories which will eventually fade and then crumble completely, pulverized by neglect.

After that, some great beings may gather up remnants of our literature, music, architecture, philosophy, love, and philanthropy -- to store them in safekeeping against the time of the next expansion of the universes, an event which is as of now by no manner of means guaranteed. If nothing survives, nothing will survive.

As I stared into space, shadows seemed to crowd around me. I was afraid of what might lie ahead for all of us.

Grand Duchess Olga of Russia

Chapter 8

Holiday in Husum

Hamburg, Germany

After returning from a stroll around the seaside village of Husum in Northern Germany, I was hungry and decided to have lunch at my hotel. By the time lunch was finished, I heard tires crunching on gravel in the driveway, followed by excited chattering from a group of newcomers. I could hear they were Americans, not the usual guests at the hotel or at the annual Festival of Piano Rarities held at the Schloss vor Husum each August. It occurred to me that the newcomers might possibly be pleasant companions during the eight-day festival.

Feeling a bit tired after lunch and wanting a nap, I passed through the lobby on the way to my room. The five new guests had registered and were ready to be shown to their rooms. They were older middle-aged, conservatively dressed, and seemed cheerful and energetic. As I passed them, we all looked at one another and nodded. I said, "Hello." They all smiled back: a conventional but friendly mutual acknowledgement. One of the women responded in a braying voice, "Well, hello back at you," and giggled loudly.

I had just seen a Trojan horse, but didn't recognize it.

Author at Sankt Peter-Ording, Germany

At age eighty-five and somewhat worldly, I continued to disappoint myself by my unguarded and naive behavior, apparently sending out welcoming and inviting signals without intention or awareness and then, as a consequence, finding myself stuck in awkward entanglements with aggressive, predatory women, or the vampires who are always cruising about looking for new victims to suck dry. (No gay men ever responded to this, whatever it was that I broadcast.) Unfortunately, I had never learned to comfortably or adequately defend myself against invasion and abuse by overly aggressive people.

We all went on to our rooms. I could hear the braying woman in the hall, so I knew the Americans were staying on my floor. I hung my Do Not Disturb sign on the doorknob and started my nap.

During the past seven years of attending the festival, I had met only a few people—a charming young Dutch man from The Hague who was fleeing a miserable love affair and an Iraqi man who had come to Germany to teach and escape the tragic situation in his homeland. Both were quiet, polite, fluent in English, and obviously interested in piano music and piano playing. During the course of previous festivals, which I attended alone, I usually had lunch once or twice with the Dutch man, but otherwise kept to myself.

The beach at Island of Sylt

Author in beach cabana, Sylt

I very seldom get lonely, and I enjoyed my time alone in Husum exploring the village, the harbor, and the Schloss; reading, playing the excellent Hamburg Steinway grand piano kept in the music room of the hotel, and working on my memoirs, which I had been writing for some time.

I came to recognize several other loners who always ate alone and walked to the concerts alone and spent the intermissions alone. Some of these people were willing to enter into a nodding relationship with me, and some were not. After the first three years of attending the festival, the elegant old German lady who sat on my left at the concerts began to exchange *Guten Abends* with me on the first night of the festival, but thereafter, not another word passed between us. Once or twice I saw her look at me with a momentary faint smile.

126

Tower in the park, Husum

127

Chopin's house Zelazowa – Wola, Poland

There was one other American, a disagreeable old professor, who did not bathe often enough and who would occasionally pass very noisy farts in the concerts and then immediately turn and glare at his neighbor, trying to shift the blame to that hapless innocent. I felt the professor was best avoided.

Many of the other audience members, apparently already acquainted, talked and laughed with one another, perhaps originally arriving together in groups, or perhaps meeting at the champagne bar set up on the grounds of the Schloss during intermissions. As I had not been drinking for more than thirty years, the champagne bar held no attraction for me. Besides, generally, I didn't want to meet anyone.

Over the course of previous festivals, each lasting about ten days, there was plenty of time for most of the group to get acquainted. The small town of Husum offered several pleasant walks and sightseeing features. The town house of the great German writer Theodor Storm was open to visitors; there was also a local historical museum. Husum is also known for a spectacular display of lavender blooming crocus in the spring.

That evening at the concert the newly arrived Americans and I nodded hello, and the next day at breakfast we introduced ourselves. They were all from Beverly Hills, frequently traveled together, and seemed to be old friends. Jimmy and Doris, very affluent-looking, had been married twenty years, a second marriage for both. They seemed devoted and comfortable with each other.

Dougie, a single man, was intelligent, jolly, and pudgy and stayed slightly apart from the others—at least he was not always with them on every excursion. He was borderline flamboyant, and I wondered if he might be gay, but I never got to know him well enough to find out. There were two single women in the group. Veronica was a widow whose husband, Jonathan, had died five years before, and I could see her sadness when she spoke of him, always lovingly.

The fifth member of the group, Maisie, was about sixty years old and heavily made up. She had bouncing dyed-blonde curls, three large diamond rings, a loud braying voice and was aggressively flirtatious. Although she was expensively and beautifully dressed, she was nowhere near as attractive as she thought she was. She said she was divorced and did not intend to remarry. In her stentorian voice, she said, "After all, I can get plenty of what I want without the bother of any ceremonies. And I don't get any complaints from my partners either." She winked at me somewhat brazenly and smiled with her mouth open slightly, showing me just the tip of her tongue. I responded by trying to look inscrutably at the fried egg on my plate.

None of the five Americans ever mentioned music or piano playing or the concerts, and I wondered what they were doing attending this very specialized and out-of-the-way event for which they demonstrated no enthusiasm or interest, although they attended every concert. I never found out the answer to this question. But I too attended every concert, finding the musical rarities fascinating and the artists, a different pianist each night, very accomplished.

On the third day of the festival, I went to my room after lunch, hung out the Do Not Disturb sign, and lay down for a rest. Thirty minutes later there was a loud knock at my door. Irritated at the disregard of my sign and my privacy, I opened the door slightly.

A hand with glossy scarlet fingernails, wearing a large diamond ring, and holding a filled wineglass angled around the door frame like a searching octopus tentacle.

A loud voice, slightly slurred, said, "I've brought you something nice—something I'm sure you'll like. We want you to join us for drinks this evening before dinner." Her tone was peremptory.

I replied to the Trojan tart, my voice expressionless, "Thank you, but I don't drink."
With that, her entire tentacle came through the door, and she said, "Oh, it's not liquor. It's only wine."

"Well, thanks anyway," I said as I started to close the door softly before she could insert any more of herself into my room. She had no choice but to withdraw the tentacle and the glass before I gently mashed them.

Harbor at Husum

After that, Maisie stared at me every day with her glittering eyes and invited me to their evening cocktail party.
Every day, I said, "Thank you, but I don't drink anymore."

Eventually, the other members of her group began to roll their eyes, impatient with Maisie's aggressive invitations. Then she started also to invite me to their postconcert get-togethers at one of the local bars. I was becoming hardened about my refusals. Her invitations continued in a steady stream. She seemed perplexed as to why I was not rushing to jump into bed with her and her bouncing curls and diamond rings. I let her continue to wonder.

One day in the hotel lobby the group was talking, and Dougie said he had received a call in the middle of the night from a friend in Beverly Hills who had forgotten about the difference in time zones. Maisie rose to the occasion and asked the young desk clerk, "When it's 6:00 p.m. in Beverly Hills, what time is it here in Husum? ... Nazi time, you know." She cackled loudly at her clever witticism and repeated it twice, louder each time. "Nazi time. When it's *Nazi time* here in Husum," she bellowed, looking triumphantly at the others.

Her friends looked uneasy, and the desk clerk looked frozen with embarrassment. The Germans are generally not amused by stupid or sarcastic references to the Nazi past.

What a gargoyle, I thought. *Talk about ugly Americans—she leads the parade.*

"Let's go," said Dougie, and they all left the lobby.

I sometimes took a stroll around the Husum harbor in the morning and noted that the morning crowd was divided into two contingents, both very solid, sturdy sybarites, mostly about one hundred pounds or more overweight, all seated at tables of the sidewalk cafes clustered around the harbor and the village square. One group was devouring gigantic chocolate sundaes; the other group was enjoying huge goblets of beer. Ice cream versus beer; it looked as if both groups were winning big time.

Two days later was the last day of the festival, and the group invited me to have dinner with them at the local Rathauskeller. I liked four of them and thought I could cope with Miss Maisie. When we were sitting down, as usual, she pushed Veronica out of the way so she could claim the chair next to mine. She was apparently still hoping she could make me her next victim. As the dinner was being served, I had a verbal exchange with Maisie and knew I had met my match with her.

131

She said in a slurred voice, "Veronica and I picked this place because we saw two very good-looking men standing outside looking it over. Maybe they were going to do repairs or eat here, or maybe they had something more interesting in mind. We didn't really know."

"Are they here?" I asked as I peered salaciously around the room.

"Who?" replied Maisie, having lost the thread of the conversation.

"The two good-looking men."

"Why are you asking about them?" Maisie enquired, seemingly puzzled.

"Because you said they were why you picked this place."

"Oh, them ... We just wanted to see how they did it."

I decided against asking, "How they did what?"

The nonsequiturs were getting too thick. I could see the conversation was about to rocket into outer space, so I concentrated on my Wiener schnitzel. Maisie continued to gabble. Her friends seemed irritated and restless. I practiced custody of the eyes, seeing only my schnitzel and its potatoes. My mouth was fully occupied with chewing, so it couldn't speak. Mercifully, the dinner was eventually over, and we all left for the final concert.

The next morning the group took off in their car for Berlin and Prague, and I went up to the music room to play the piano and sooth my somewhat jangled self.

Should I try Husum again next year?

Probably. The music is good.

Chapter 9

Next Year in Husum

Over many years I had enjoyed my visits to the Husum Festival of Piano Rarities held at the Schloss vor Husum every August.

Schloss vor Husum)

133

The Schloss itself is a beautiful historic building set in a park close to the center of Husum, a charming old fishing village in Northern Germany located about one hundred miles north of Hamburg and about fifty miles south of the famous resort of Sylt, an island in the North Sea known for its nude beaches, and only about fifty miles farther to the Danish border.

Schlossgarten

I went to have a look at Sylt once and was impressed by the steady cold wind blowing off the North Sea—there were two unclothed people sitting forlornly on the sand. The inhabitants of the sleek modern hotels and cozy villas had all chosen to stay inside that day.

The concert hall at Husum, a large oblong room on the second floor of the Schloss, seats 160 with a connecting smaller room holding about fifty seats for overflow guests. Unfortunately, the concert hall is not air-conditioned, and if the windows are left open for ventilation, there is an occasional ruckus from the ducks swimming on the moat surrounding the Schloss; if the windows are closed, it soon becomes quite hot in the hall. Sometimes the pianists look like they are getting overheated. (It's hard physical work playing a piano concert.) At least there are no mosquitoes. I too occasionally found myself quite uncomfortable from the heat during the performances. The concerts are recorded, and a CD of highlights of the festival's performances is issued a few months after the end of the event. The directors of the event feel that any quacking ducks on the recordings would be inappropriate; I think they would be charming and reminiscent of this special place and event.

Street scene, Husum

Ten or so pianists perform each year, a different pianist each evening. They are mostly European with a sprinkling of Americans and Asians, generally in the early to middle stages of their careers, although some are quite famous. Marc-André Hamelin, in my opinion one of the world's foremost pianists, performs every other year, and many of the others are quite well known. All are extremely fine artists.

135

Street scene, Husum

Flower market, Husum

Husum market

I have never heard anything less than expert performances from artists such as Paul Badura-Skoda, Carlo Grante, Stephen Hough, Piers Lane, Martin Jones, Alexei Lubimov, Hamish Milne, Ronald Smith, Roberto Szidon, and Nina Tichman, among others—a stellar roster. The recitals are uniformly sold out, with no empty seats in the hall, and usually the overflow room is also filled. The programs are composed mostly of unusual piano compositions, the rarities announced in the series title. Any pianist who played an all-Beethoven sonata program, for instance, would never be invited again to participate in this series. The attentive audiences are composed of serious lovers of piano music who travel to this relatively out-of-the-way location to experience what they love.

Husum has a very fine hotel, the Romantik Hotel Altes Gymnasium, reputedly the best hotel in Northern Germany—truly a very comfortable and elegant establishment, with a one-starred Michelin restaurant and a beautiful swimming pool, much like the Paris Ritz.

All in all, the Husum Festival was always a great pleasure to attend. But nothing is perfect, and I recalled the 2013 event when I was pestered by the extremely forward American woman, Maisie, obviously on the search for a new victim/husband. Because many of the guests at the festival stay at the Altes Gymnasium Hotel in Husum, we were often all in the hotel dining room at the same time for meals.

After the end of the previous year's festival, I was so irritated by Maisie's brazen pursuit that I had considered not attending the festival again this year. But in the interval I had changed my mind, thinking, *Why should I penalize myself by cancelling one of the nicest events of my year just so as to avoid Maisie the octopus? I can handle/avoid her. And perhaps she won't attend the festival again this year.*

The first evening when we were all having dinner, I saw with relief that Maisie was not present, and it turned out that she indeed did not attend this year's event. What a relief! Little did I suspect how harmless and innocent little Miss Maisie would come to appear.

The programs looked very interesting this year and got off to a good start. The old grand dame, who attends the festival every year, saw me come in and take my usual seat next to hers in the auditorium. She gave me her standard curt nod and frosty, "Guten Abend." Last year, every evening when I came in and sat down, I said to her, "Guten Abend," but received no reply, not even a glance. After that, I never looked at her or spoke to her again. It bothers me to be so rude, but I decided not to give her the pleasure of cutting me dead every evening. I noticed that she usually spoke to a few select people each evening, usually at intermission, but she always had a displeased, haughty expression. She must be a lady of highest rank, at least a princess if not an empress. I noticed that my reaction to her rudeness was a combination of amusement and irritation. Perhaps she disliked Americans ... or men ... or bald people—her right. I didn't like her either; so there!

I recognized some of the people from previous years: the young Dutch man, the Iraqi teacher, the Japanese man, the sourpuss American professor from New York, and Gudrun and Paolo, a German couple from Dortmund. All seemed enthusiastic about the beginning of the festival.

A common meeting place was the dining room, located between two wings of the hotel. The room had many large windows, so anyone passing by had a clear view of the interior and the diners at their tables. From the first breakfast this season, we all resumed our previous year's dining room habits—some coming alone and sitting by themselves; others coming in pairs or larger groups. Many of the diners nodded and spoke. Some were very cordial and always sat in groups; others preferred to be alone.

The diners were generally a sedate group. There was some drinking at lunch and dinner, but the conversation was generally quiet, nothing rowdy, sometimes punctuated by vigorous laughter. Over the course of the festival, most guests spoke at least sometimes to all the other guests, and we all seemed to some extent to feel part of the group. After breakfast, several of the guests usually lingered for a while, drinking coffee and talking. There were also chairs and settees outside on the hotel's grounds, under large old spreading trees; sometimes some of the guests would sit there for a while. The ambience was very pleasant.

On the second day, Gudrun and Paolo came in for breakfast and joined me at my table. I was happy to see them again, and we had a chat catching up on what had happened since we last met.

Paolo, about forty-five years old, was trim and athletic, about five feet ten inches, handsome, with blue eyes and salt-and-pepper hair. He was a lawyer from Trieste, obviously intelligent, quiet, and soft-spoken. He was serious but pleasant. Gudrun, his wife, also about forty-five with black hair and dark eyes, was from sophisticated and elegant Berlin. She was quite overweight but surprisingly quick and determined in her movements. A school administrator, she was pleasant to talk with but had an intense expression, and sometimes her face could assume an angry appearance, almost frightening in its severity and hostility. She favored tight black silk clothes, which added to a rather sinister effect. They both spoke English perfectly, and it was a relief to me to talk to people freely without lots of censorship and simplification.

We had a meal together about every other day, whenever we met by chance in the dining room. They were friendly and sociable and seemed to enjoy my company and usually sat down at my table if I was there first, or they invited me to sit with them if they were first. Gudrun especially seemed to be becoming more enthusiastic about me, smiling broadly and sometimes talking in a low, conspiratorial voice, as though we were plotting something.

On the way home from the concert one evening, a distance of about a quarter of a mile, I heard footsteps behind me, hurrying, as if trying to catch up. I heard a voice calling my name: "Johni Schaatzi, Johni Schaatzi, wait up." Soon Gudrun was at my side, smiling and nodding. "How did you like the concert this evening?" she asked.

We walked home the rest of the way together, talking of musical matters and that evening's music. When we reached the hotel's grounds, Gudrun took my arm in a very strong grasp and said, "I'm sorry we have to say good night now. Maybe tomorrow we can do something more." She pulled me brusquely toward her, using both hands. She was so forceful I almost lost my balance.
I didn't want to pursue this further, so I just said casually, "See you tomorrow." I then turned away and went into the hotel. I felt somewhat uneasy but dismissed the matter. I didn't see them at breakfast the next day.

The next afternoon was rainy, and I sat in the lobby of the hotel reading. Paolo and Gudrun came in and sat down close to me in a small group of chairs.

Gudrun began to speak. "We went to the most interesting place yesterday. Have you been there? It's only about five miles down the road, in the garden of a beautiful villa. The garden is carefully planted and maintained, and in the middle of the garden is a large globe, about fifteen feet in diameter. It is made of wood and plaster. There is a locked door on one side of the globe, but we had been given a key by the gardener. When we opened the door, we could see inside. There were two very comfortable sofas and six or so large hassocks or pillows scattered about the floor. There were several windows about eight feet above the floor, so there was plenty of light, and also privacy. We locked the door from inside and then started relaxing on the sofas. The room was so romantic and sexy that we soon found ourselves getting even more comfortable. And then we did it a second time. Very interesting experience. I can't wait to show it to you. When would you like to go there? Now? *Now?*"

"Well, I am expecting a phone call, so thanks for the invitation, but I have to stay here. I had better go to my room now to wait for the call." I began to have the feeling that a plot was developing or at least a setup, and somehow I was the prize. I am very uneasy about such matters, having a keen nose for traps. Also, I found neither Gudrun nor Paolo to my sexual liking and didn't consider myself in play that way.

"Oh, I am very sorry you have to leave so early," Gudrun said, leering slightly. "We hope we see you tomorrow."

"Oh, yes," I murmured and then scuttled up to my room and locked myself in, safe and protected.

At the concert that evening, Paolo came over to me and said, "Gudrun wants you to join us and some of our friends after the concert at the Storm Hotel." (I knew it to be a pleasant hotel, close to the Schloss, named after the Husum writer Theodor Storm.)

"Thanks, Paolo, but I can't do it tonight. I'm expecting a friend to drop by."

On the way home from the concert that evening, I could hear accelerating footsteps behind me. I sped up my walking. The steps behind me broke into a run and came closer, and I assumed they would soon pass me by. Not at all! Suddenly, there was a very strong blow on my back, making me stagger and almost knocking me over.

"What the hell," I yelled.

A large black form passed me and then stopped. Almost screaming with laughter, Gudrun turned around to face me, both her hands clenched in fists.

"Just a little surprise for you. Did you like it?"

"No, not at all," I said sternly, continuing to walk toward the hotel.

Gudrun walked the other way, back toward the Schloss.

The next afternoon Gudrun invited me to join them and their friends for drinks after the concert, and I stupidly accepted.

That evening I went to the bar at the Storm Hotel, and there were Paolo and Gudrun and eight of their friends, only two of whom spoke English. They were mostly laborers such as carpenters, delivery men, etc. and were no match for their hosts in social standing or sophistication. They all seemed surprised that I did not drink, which gave rise to a few of the usual questions as to why not. After about an hour of forced and desultory conversation, I excused myself, thanked our hosts, and went home. This seemed a strange and pointless encounter, entertaining no one. I did not understand why it seemed so important to Gudrun that I should join them, but I had some suspicions.

The next afternoon I was again reading in the hotel lobby. Gudrun and Paolo came in and marched up to me. "We're here to take you to the globe," Gudrun said flatly, fixing me with a basilisk's stare.

"So sorry. I have some work I must finish this afternoon. But thanks anyway," I said.

They both scowled, and Gudrun particularly looked angry. I went upstairs to my room. By this time I was beginning to be afraid of them. What did all this pressure mean? Her hitting me so hard on the way home, their push that I should join them and their friends for a drink, and now this insistence that I should sit inside a locked garden sphere with them, a place where they'd had sex.

I had begun to suspect that Gudrun might be a stalker and perhaps could escalate into becoming vicious and dangerous. Because of events in my earlier life, and because of events in my psychiatric training and practice, I have become trusting of my fear responses. At any rate, I had no inclination to disregard my responses so as to humor this very aggressive and inappropriate woman.

The next day, as most were checking out and leaving the hotel, they were passing through the lobby, and I said, "Good-bye. Bon voyage."

Gudrun replied, "When I first see you at next year's festival, I insist on taking you to our garden globe." She then scowled at me and said in an ominous and vicious-sounding growl, "*And I won't take no for an answer.*" Her lips were pulled back from her teeth in a snarl, and her face didn't show the least trace of a smile.

I knew from her voice and expression this was no pleasantry, or much less a joke. It was a serious, grim threat. Not knowing what she might do next, I said, "Well, let's see," and I was careful not to turn my back to her while she was still in the room.

I wondered if I had done something to project a naive innocence or something other to serve as an invitation to this couple. Perhaps they were sadists trolling for a new victim.

What should I do? As much as I liked the festival, I resolved not to attend again, because I was terrified of her.

Luckily, my friend Steve offered to accompany me to the Husum festival the following year, so I would have protection against Gudrun.

Husum market and Husum Flower Market (below)

Café in Husum

Chapter 10

We Visit a Grand Duchess

The day after the festival ended Steve and I drove to Hamburg and checked in at the Vier Jahreszeiten Hotel, where I had stayed several times before. It stands on the shore of the Inner Alster Lake and has a good view of the town, the water fountains in the lake, and the various boats going back and forth. The elevated dining room offered both delicious food and an excellent view.

We had decided to drive to Berlin so as to see Northern Germany, as well as the gigantic Schwerin Palace built on a few islands in Lake Schwerin. It had been allowed to dilapidate for fifty years under the Russian and then the East German regimes following the end of the Second World War. I had heard it was still being refurbished and wondered if it might be regaining its former glory (like the beautiful rehabilitation of the Residenz Palace in Wurzburg).

The grand dukes of Mecklenburg-Schwerin had been among the richest and most powerful of the German princes, and Schwerin had been their capital. There had been considerable intermarriage between the princely houses of Mecklenburg and the Russian royal family.

Before the Russian revolution, although the czar was the head of the Romanov dynasty, his elder cousins and uncles were also very powerful. The czar's aunt, Her Imperial Highness the Grand

Duchess Maria Pavlovna the Elder, Grand Duchess of Mecklenburg-Schwerin(1854-1920), known in the family as Aunt Miechen (also known as Ducky), had married the senior Romanov Grand Duke Vladimir Alexandrovich (1874–1909), the son of the Emperor Alexander II and the beloved Empress Marie Alexandrovna. Grand Duke Vladimir was interested in art and literature and had amassed a fine collection of paintings by the most eminent Russian artists.

Schwerin Palace

After the revolution and the murder of Czar Nicholas and the imperial family, the Grand Duke Vladimir's son, Cyril proclaimed himself emperor of Russia. His claim was neither seconded nor opposed by other members of the family. The Dowager Empress Marie, the late czar's mother and head of the family, was not supportive of the Grand Duke's son and his mother, Aunt Miechen's claim. Aunt Miechen felt superior to the current Empress Alexandra Feodorovna; they quite disliked each other.

Aunt Miechen had one of the finest private jewel collections in the world, rivaled only by the state collections of the Queen of England, the Shah of Iran, and the Maharajah of Baroda, owner of the fabled Golconda diamond mine.

Aunt Miechen's famous emeralds, known as the Cambridge emeralds, had once belonged to Catherine the Great (and later on to the Duchess of Cambridge and then on to Barbara Hutton, the much-married Woolworth heiress, and then to Elizabeth Taylor, the famous and beautiful American actress).

Someone who was present at the engagement party of Barbara Hutton told the author that she had been wearing the emeralds at the dinner party. Unfortunately, she'd had too much to drink, and as her head gradually and slowly descended toward her dinner plate, the fabled emerald necklace of Catherine the Great also descended until her head and the emerald necklace were both lying on her plate in a pool of mashed potatoes and gravy.

The emeralds survived the dinner party and were easily cleaned, but Miss Hutton's dignity needed some refurbishment.

Hotel du Palais, Biarritz
Gift of Emperor Napoleon III to Empress Eugenie

Aunt Miechen also owned the so-called Vladimir Tiara, composed of loops of diamonds with large pearl or diamond or emerald drops (interchangeable) in the center of each loop. A few years later, after the revolution, many of Aunt Miechen's jewels were sold; the stunning Vladimir Tiara and some other items were purchased by Queen Mary of England. They were later inherited by Queen Elizabeth II of England, and the queen is occasionally photographed wearing the tiara, which becomes the queen, and the queen, in return, becomes the tiara—a happy combination. Aunt Miechen also owned a brilliant ruby parure that had once belonged to Napoleon's Empress Josephine.

(
The beach at Biarritz

The Vladimirs maintained a court that rivaled the imperial court a few yards away on the St. Petersburg palace embankment. It was sometimes said to be more splendid than the imperial court. Aunt Miechen formerly had a hospital train during the Great War, which had transported wounded soldiers from the front to hospitals in St. Petersburg and Moscow.

Author in coffee house, Marseilles

Even after the Russian revolution, Aunt Miechen was able to maintain her private train, an amazing feat. Her haughty and imperious bearing enabled her to give orders to many people, who reflexively obeyed. She was, of course, not widely liked, but her situation was improved by the fact that she was the sister of Queen Marie of Romania, who was generally admired and respected.

After the revolution, Aunt Miechen and her family were able to escape Russia in 1917 on an Italian steamer, going first to Venice and then on to Switzerland and France, settling in the town of Saint-Briac-sur-Mer. She visited America, where she was received with full royal honors. Back home in St. Briac she was able to help her financial situation by painting and selling her own beautiful small paintings of flowers.

Grand Duke Vladimir's and Aunt Miechen's son, Cyril Vladimirovich (1876–1938), later on claimed the throne and announced that he was the rightful czar. The other family members, particularly the Dowager Empress Marie, did not recognize him as

Large topiary dog, Guggenheim Museum, Bilbao

head of the family, so they were, in effect, denying his claim to be the czar. Aunt Miechen was, of course, furious, but she was clearly outranked in the family by the dowager empress, so she had to remain quiet.

But, if Vladimir were the czar and then died (as he did in 1909), his son Cyril would become the next czar. Aunt Miechen noted immediately that she might then become the Czarina of Russia, and she left no time in proclaiming herself to be the empress. The family laughed about this preening.

In 1924 Cyril proclaimed himself emperor, even though no one in the family supported his claim. However, Cyril was the first of the major Russian nobility to sign a document pledging his allegiance to the new revolutionary government. In all these machinations, Aunt Miechen was so grandiose and irritable that no one dared to contradict her.

As years passed and the family was not restored to the throne, she became more disappointed and bitter and finally died in St. Briac in 1920, so Aunt Miechen was therefore removed from the imperial family's roster.

The Dowager Empress Marie died in 1928 while staying at her home in Denmark as a guest of her brother, the King of Denmark. Her sister, Queen Alexandra of England, was often with her, but they became less close in their old ages, particularly after Queen Alexandra began showing signs of advancing senility.

A great granddaughter of Vladimir, the Grand Duchess Maria Vladimirovna, is the current claimant to the throne of Russia. It is unknown whether the monarchy might someday be restored so the grand duchess might ascend the throne. There is some slight interest inside Russia in restoring the monarchy. Currently (2016), that doesn't seem very likely, but the future, no doubt, holds many surprises.

Steve and I had had a very good time at the piano festival in Husum, and we looked forward to driving through Northern Germany and finishing our trip with a few days in Berlin.

The first part of the drive was through the coastal plains of Mecklenburg, home to multitudes of sheep and cattle. After about three hours of driving, we passed Lübeck, and then we began to see a huge structure on the horizon. Coming closer, we could recognize the Schwerin Palace, tall, bulky, and with many turrets, very impressive and picturesque, built on several islands in the Schwerin Lake.

We drove into the center of Schwerin, parked the car, and walked over to the palace where we bought tickets and entered. I felt a shiver of apprehension.

As we went through the various rooms of the palace, an unearthly silence seemed to settle over the place, and the quality of the light inside the palace also seemed to change, becoming a not quite fully transparent lavender. There was a faint fragrance of tuberoses and lilies. No people were to be seen, which seemed odd for the middle of the visiting hours.

Continuing our tour of the palace, we entered a small room with a fireplace, beautiful tapestries, and elegant French eighteenth-century furniture. In the dim light we could just make out that a lady was sitting on one of the settees, crying quietly. Not wanting to intrude, but being extremely curious (almost desperately so) as to who she was and why she was crying, we quietly approached the sobbing woman.

I was familiar with portraits and photographs of many of the major Romanovs of the past century, and I was shocked to recognize the lady, dressed elaborately in an old-fashioned style, as the Grand Duchess Maria Pavlovna the Elder, Aunt Miechen herself. As she was the Grand Duchess of Mecklenburg-Schwerin (in her own right), this was one of her own palaces, and she appeared comfortable and at home in this very grand residence even though she had died almost a hundred years earlier.

She noticed us looking at her and gave us a brief but cordial nod.

"Good morning, Your Highness," we said.

"Good morning, young sirs," replied the grand duchess.

"Please favor me by telling me your names."

"I am John Loomis, and this is my friend Steve. We are both from New York and are taking a tour of Europe. We couldn't help but notice your tears. Is there anything we can do to help you?"

GD: "Well, I am uncertain as to what may have been happening here. We have not had any visitors for a very long time.

There have been no servants here, and no mail has arrived. Can you explain these strange events?"

JL: "Your Highness, we have serious news for you and an explanation of your current situation. Sometimes, when people are very worried about something, they overlook important events. We are sorry to tell you that you died in 1920, more than ninety years ago. Your passing was so tranquil that you did not notice. You have stayed here, in your sheltering palace, ever since, disoriented and fearful. Has no one told you what you need to do next?"

GD: "Oh my! What a terrible shock! Are you sure about this? Or perhaps you are only teasing me. How could it be? Am I really dead? Am I in heaven?" She began to sob again. We sat down near her and continued to talk with her.

I remembered what I had been told to do in this situation when I was studying at the Monroe Institute a few years earlier. I mentally broadcast a call for two helpers to take care of and help the grand duchess, noting that she was a very grand and rigid and haughty person but basically had a good heart. She had been stuck in the transition phase of her existence and was in desperate need of help to move on to the next stage of her afterlife. I did not know how to guide her myself, as I was still one of the living and not well acquainted with the pathways and stations of the immediate after-death territory.

JL: "Your Highness, did you ever hear Franz Liszt or Anton Rubinstein play the piano?"

GD: "Yes, and I knew them both well. Liszt was such a cavalier and so attractive. I felt very drawn to him. And when he played. Oh my! I was so thrilled I almost fainted when I let him kiss my hand. And Anton Rubinstein—very brooding, but so magnetic, almost threatening in his attractiveness. You know, of course, that I created the conservatory in St. Petersburg for him, and I appointed him to be the first director there. It was unfortunate that his brother Nicholas was so jealous and disagreeable, even though he was the director of the conservatory in Moscow."

Behold, the two great pianists entered the room, giving kindly looks to the duchess and a cordial greeting to each other, and a quick nod to Steve and me..

JL: "Madame, there is nothing for you to be afraid of. I think you will find the short tour arranged by these two great artists interesting and reassuring. And you may expect to see many of your loved ones waiting for you. Your Highness, here are two of your admirers, who have come to help guide you to your next destination. May I present Anton Rubinstein and Franz Liszt, whom you have met before in your palace in St. Petersburg?"

GD: "I am happy to see you both again. Before we go on with the tour you are planning for me, could I request that you each play the piano for me?"

Anton Rubinstein: "Your Highness, I remember when you were studying the piano with me at your own conservatory in St. Petersburg. You had great talent and sensitivity. I hope you have continued your diligent practice so as to give much pleasure to yourself and to those around you. It would be a great honor to play for you. Here is my composition 'Rêve Angélique.'"

There was a splendid Bechstein grand piano in the room, and he played this divine music for us. I had never before heard any music so beautiful; we all had tears in our eyes. The grand duchess thanked him very graciously, commenting his playing made her resolved to practice harder at the piano. Rubinstein smiled and nodded.

Franz Liszt: He was dressed all in black in abbé's clothing, looking like a dark angel with his halo of white hair. "I remember very well meeting you at the Comtesse d'Agoult's villa in Nice, Your Highness. I was entranced by your beauty, grace, and intelligence and thought of you for many weeks afterward. I had hoped to meet you more intimately but had no idea that we would have to wait almost a century for our next meeting."

GD: "And I felt the same about you. I was too shy to let you know my feelings. But now that a hundred years have passed and we are all much wiser and stronger, I am ashamed and apologize for not letting you know my feelings."

FL: "Well, here we are, and off to a better start this time. Now I will play you my 'God's Benediction in the Solitude.'" Liszt's performance of this magnificent and spiritually inspired composition left us all speechless and deeply moved.

These two pieces were perfectly chosen for beginning the grand duchess's introductory tour of the next world, and she thanked the artists graciously for their beautiful performances.

The two great pianists stretched out their hands to her, and she gave each man one of her hands, the right to Rubinstein and the left hand to Liszt. Linked, they all three turned and walked toward the door of the little room. The grand duchess was dressed in her most magnificent Russian court costume, complemented by her magnificent emerald parure, her rubies, and the beautiful Vladimir Tiara sparkling in the candlelight. She looked serenely regal, like an angel on earth.

Just before they went through the door, she turned and exclaimed in rapture, "There they all are, smiling, holding out their hands and waving in welcome. Even Grandmama Queen has come to greet me! I am so happy now. All my sorrows have been erased."

The three turned as if to exit the room but instead slowly faded away. The great pianists had guided the grand duchess to the next step in her afterlife process. We were very moved and realized our work at the palace had been completed. It was time for us to leave.

Saluting the scene, we left the palace, found the car, and started our drive to the city. In a couple of hours we arrived at the Adlon Hotel in Berlin, turned our car over to the doorman, and were shown to our beautiful rooms.

Grand Duchess Marie Pavlovna

Chapter 11

Havana after Midnight

At two o'clock in the morning, dressed in his gauzy yellow nightdress, Ignacio lay on his back on the smooth silk sheets that covered the big bed he had sent back from Paris years ago. Although it was only March, the weather in Havana was already quite warm, and Buca, one of his favorite slaves, had been pulling the punkah rope for the past two hours.

Ignacio was thinking about the big party planned for the next day in honor of his fifty-fifth birthday, to be attended by Havana society and foreign dignitaries, as was only fitting. After all, he was Ignacio Cervantes, leading pianist and composer of Cuba, world famous, the friend of Gioachino Rossini, Charles Gounod, and Franz Liszt.

Even so, more mundanely, he wished Cuba would modernize, join the twentieth century, and install electricity like they have in New York and Paris, so he could enjoy more reliable fanning than was provided by Buca. It was already 1902, and Cuba should stop blaming its lack of progress on the Spanish-American war and Cuba's own civil war.

The doors to the terrace were wide open. The powerful fragrance of jasmine was floating in like a sweet memory from a happy time.

He heard his name being called softly. "Nacio? Nacio?"

Ignacio Cervantes

He looked toward the terrace and saw a flickering form beginning to materialize in the doorway. He was terrified. Buca gave a loud gasp and then sucked in his breath in fear, his eyes opening wider than anyone could have imagined possible. He began to pull the punkah rope at double speed.

"Nacio, dear, I mean you no harm. You have no need to be afraid. You know who I am." The form continued to become more definite, and Ignacio began to recognize someone familiar. Could it be? Could it be his old friend? Was it really her? His old love? It was a dream come true, and his heart soared. He was full of joy for the first time in many years, and the ache in his heart disappeared.

He was not afraid, but he was shocked, surprised, and delighted to see his dear old Parisian friend, Marceline, the Princess

Czartoryska, entering his room. He thought she looked very well, very lovely, even though she would now be eighty-two years old had she not died about twenty years earlier.

At first he was speechless, but then he pulled himself together and said, "You look lovelier than ever, my dear Marceline. What a wonderful surprise to see you. How are you?"

"I was concerned about you and wanted to pay you a visit to see for myself. It's so hot here I can hardly stand it. It would kill me if I stayed here very long. So to speak, of course. Please pardon the figure of speech. At any rate, you look quite dissipated—I'm shocked. I've heard reports ... Your vigor declines as your career rises.

"I remember when you were captivating and quite tireless. Your gauzy yellow nightgown is a disgrace—more fit for a courtesan than for you. What has become of you? Are you no longer a champion sexual virtuoso? Do you remember all the tricks and charms I taught you? I think you may need my six-month refresher course in wholesome living," she laughed.

Well, the princess was always one to come to the point. It began to seem that the visit might be an attempt to resurrect former ecstasies. Ignacio smiled as he recalled the old days.

He had won first prize at the Paris Conservatory, where he had been the star pupil of both Professor Marmontel and the great pianist Charles-Valentin Alkan. After he graduated in 1866, the Parisian musical world of great composers and fashionable salons welcomed him. At age eighteen, he was an eager pupil of the life of pleasure, wanting to taste the worldly delights which the elegant and aristocratic Parisians were happy to share with him.

Handsome and blazingly talented, he had wavy brown hair and soft dark eyes that occasionally glittered with excitement or anticipation of pleasure. Well built, radiating charm and animal eagerness, tireless and enthusiastic, if not very sophisticated sexually, he was naturally much desired as an adornment for the best salons and bedrooms. All doors sprang open as he approached.

For Ignacio, these brilliant Parisian characters seemed full of promise. One woman above all others fascinated him—the beautiful Princess Marceline Czartoryska. Her perfect features and flawless skin; large, sparkling blue eyes; very light brown hair; and voluptuous figure, combined with a radiant smile, great charm, and an air of mystery, intrigue, and gaiety, had brought all Paris to her feet. She was twenty-seven years older than Ignacio and was the most admired woman in Paris.

It was rumored that she had even been offered the favors of the emperor himself, which she had charmingly declined. Her husband, the prince, had died in a duel some years earlier, leaving her his huge Polish estates. She was enormously rich, beautiful, sophisticated, and at the peak of her physical exuberance and had a well-deserved reputation for flamboyance.

As a teenager she had been a student of the famous piano teacher Carl Czerny in Paris. When she was twenty-eight, in 1848, she had been one of the last, best, and favorite pupils of Frédéric Chopin. After they became accustomed to the roles of teacher and pupil, they discovered a fondness and strong physical attraction, and so eventually, their relationship swelled to the point of including giving one another serene, soft strokings to the point of extreme pleasure. Chopin was too ill by then, one year before his death from consumption, to function fully as her lover.

She was, of course, naturally discreet about the relationship. As a token of his fondness and gratitude for her loving companionship, he gave her several of his manuscript scores with his own interpretive markings and fingerings. Part of the mystique of Chopin's music was his belief that each finger had a distinctive voice, and he was very particular as to which fingering was best in any passage of his compositions, so his instruction was invaluable, particularly in the interpretation of his own compositions.

One of the best pianists in Paris, Marceline played both of Chopin's concertos and many of his other compositions, and her playing was much admired. She took great pleasure in performing the works Frédéric had given her. It was said by many that of all Chopin's students, her playing was the most like her master's, with exquisite interpretations, beautiful tone, and infinite nuances.

She had been one of the four ladies who were with him at the end, in 1849, in his rooms on the Place Vendôme, when she held him lovingly in her arms as he died. She was in mourning for a long time after Chopin had passed away—she had really loved him.

Marceline

Later on, in 1854, she had gone on a visit to see the French ambassador to Burma who was living in Mandalay, the imperial city. She was presented at the Burmese court to King Mindon, the young, handsome, and progressive ruler of Burma.

He soon invited her to join his court. There she learned many secret tricks, charms, potions, and sweet surprises from the king, but fortunately remained kindly and fun-loving. She learned to make her beautiful mouth, with its soft lips, hard teeth, and firm tongue, an organ for giving and receiving exquisite pleasures, and before long the king fell in love with Marceline.

The king eventually came under dangerous pressure from the queen to send the princess away. The queen, sometimes called the

Tiger, was known to have removed several of those whom she considered obstacles or rivals by using the services of her personal poisoner.

King Mindon of Mandalay

So Marceline and the king eventually said good-bye with loving regret, leaving each other with heavily perfumed memories. As a parting gift, the king gave her six exquisite golden hair ornaments encrusted with diamonds, rubies, and pearls. In later years she sometimes wore them at her own grander parties and on other very special occasions.

After her return to Paris, it was reliably rumored that she sometimes kept an outstandingly attractive young man voluntarily locked in her boudoir to serve as her willing sexual devotee. The term for this voluptuous imprisonment was six months (unless the young man turned out to be a disappointment, in which case he would be dismissed earlier).

After this glorious term was over, Marceline would give her young lover a final kiss and a very generous souvenir before sending him on his way. None of the young men wanted to be expelled or to leave her paradise. All of them remained her loyal friends, and none ever forgot his time with her.

She would then spend a few weeks at Baden-Baden to refresh her spirit as well as her body, sparkling each night as she attended the casino, wagering large sums and laughing whether she won or lost. Being charming as well as beautiful and very rich, she attracted around her a stellar group of people. She especially enjoyed the company of several Russian grand dukes, as well as the companionship of the Princess Bonaparte, a leader of Parisian society.

Shortly after she returned home from her most recent stay at the spa, she was invited to a gala party to which Ignacio had also been invited. He played his own compositions—the Cuban Danzas, which captivated all who were present, especially the ladies, with musical hints of strange melancholy. The ladies felt insistent stirrings of prurient passions as they listened to the handsome young man play.

Ignacio was presented to the princess for the first time.

They had difficulty hiding their immediate strong attraction and excitement, and each recognized that the other held a promise of ecstasy. Within a few weeks, they had developed a closeness, and Ignacio was joyously locked into Marceline's boudoir as her new and happily eager sex magnet.

As they practiced their respective strengths and talents, the promise of ecstasies was fulfilled. It would be difficult to say which of them was the toy and which the toyer. They were both extremely beautiful, and although Marceline was forty-five years old, age had not yet begun to make its marks on her. Of course, at eighteen Ignacio was just approaching the peak of his ripeness.

A Pleyel piano was in the boudoir, and Marceline played Chopin for him. Her playing was exquisite, just as Chopin himself had taught her. Ignacio played his own Danzas for her and taught her some of them. Their six months floated by dreamily, with increasing sexual ecstasy, much music, rest, good food, and generally radiant happiness.

Marceline continued to go to parties, but only rarely; all her friends knew she was in love again and so did not press her. At the end of the six months, both Marceline and Ignacio were surprised to want to extend their paradise for another six months, which turned out to be even happier than the first term.

But at the end of the year, they both knew they must move on to a different life; destiny commanded it. They knew that if they lingered further, the gods of love would tear them to shreds for their presumption, and so with the most extreme regret and affection, they said good-bye.

Ignacio gave her his newest and most beautiful Danza, dedicated, of course, to Marceline; and she gave him her Chopin scores, which were his greatest treasure from then on. After that, they met occasionally at parties. They yearned for each other but knew they could not chance the turbulence of another sexual encounter without being shaken to pieces by their passion. Two years later, in 1869, Ignacio had to return to Havana.

Many women in Havana smiled at Ignacio and made their interest plain, but he was in thrall to Marceline's memory and felt that he was somehow waiting for her. He remained alone, devoting himself to his music and his memories. As he would play, he sometimes entered a reverie and became one with his memories of the past. Marceline's beauty floated over them.

In 1882, at the age of 62, Marceline died in Paris during a typhoid epidemic. Her kindness, elegance, generosity, and sparkling charm were a serious loss to Parisian society. When Ignacio heard of her death, he was bereft and wept many tears.

He continued to wait for her, not exactly realizing what he was doing, but he felt somehow he would see her again. And now it had come to pass. Thirty-five years after their last meeting, Marceline was here, in Havana, more beautiful than ever, full of sparkle and excitement.

"I would love to hear you play your Danzas again," she said.

And so they went downstairs to the music room. Buca was still very afraid, but managed with shaking hands to light some candles, and Marceline and Ignacio sat down side by side on the piano bench. As he played for her, he tried to express in music his love for her—that he had never forgotten her, that he still yearned for her. Then he asked her to play Chopin for him. With an exquisite, silvery tone and a most nuanced and refined legato, Marceline played a nocturne and two waltzes.

"I see you have not lost your beautiful touch," he said.

"Well, in this afterlife state there is no deterioration of any kind. One's abilities just get better, even without any practice," she said.

Standing close together and with their faces almost touching, Marceline put her right hand gently over his left ear and looked straight into his eyes. She quietly and seriously said, "Nacio, dear, I still love you very much."

Nacio was struck almost unconscious. He felt something crumble and break inside himself, releasing a flood of feelings he had not known for many years. His love instantly became an irresistible torrent, sweeping him away to a new existence. Shivers of pleasure began running up his spine from a point between his shoulder blades to burst inside his head. His skin was pushed outward by thousands of sparkling points of heat. The bones in his fingers trembled first with excitement and then with ecstasy. His tender and lonely heart, which had lain comatose for so many years as if in the deepest recesses of a dark cave, suddenly awakened into a land of brilliant colors, intoxicating perfumes, and swirling clouds of love. His eyes could suddenly see in all directions at once. His beautiful new world was welcoming him on every side.

He knew that this was the most important moment of his life—that he must not make a mistake, that this was his final chance for real happiness. He did not know the words to carry his feelings. Terrified, overjoyed, and with deepest humility, Nacio answered Marceline and whispered, "Yes ... Love."

The irresistible force of their long-suppressed passion caused the massive, invisible gate between life and death to swing slowly and softly open. He could feel his cold, rigid soul turn molten, and a hot new world began to form itself inside him.

Marceline murmured, "I only have another hour before I have to go back. Why don't we go upstairs again?" And so they returned to Ignacio's bedroom.

Ignacio shyly took off his clothes, realizing their previous age difference was now almost exactly reversed. He knew how out of shape he had become. His days as a young Adonis had faded long ago, although they both remembered that time well.

Marceline said, "When I see you standing there waiting for me, I remember the ecstasy and exaltation you gave me so many times. You are as beautiful and desirable to me now as you were thirty-five years ago."

As Marceline began to reveal herself, Ignacio was stunned to see that she had the body of a twenty-five-year-old woman: firm breasts, flat stomach, and strong thighs. She was more glorious than he had ever known. Seeing his surprised admiration, she said, "In this afterlife state we soon return to the time of life when we were in our most perfect physical condition. But I do wish I had the golden hairpins King Mindon gave me. I know you always liked me to wear them for you at special times, like now." They both smiled softly.

They slowly and fervently embraced, and their bodies rejoiced and remembered all the old ecstasies. Through their skin and through their mouths, each could feel the excitement and joy of the other. Their spirits fused, became one instead of two, became incandescent, and were surrounded by a glittering white light. Their bodies touching and their souls united, they left this world and floated in rapture on a sea of love and bliss. They were bathed in pulsating music and in the scintillating colors of the rainbow. Their union moved above space and time. Eternity was theirs.

When they finished their lovemaking, they slowly and softly parted again, this time safe in the knowledge that their union would endure and sustain them, life after life, age after age, forever. After that, they were separated by only the thinnest of veils between their two worlds.

Ignacio could sometimes hear Marceline playing Chopin or her own special Danza and could hear her voice calling him. Marceline continued to wait for Ignacio and could sometimes dimly see him waiting on the other side and could hear his voice calling to her.

After enduring three more years of yearning, the veil between them was removed forever.

Dedicated to all the orphan memories crying to come home.

Author's friend, concert violinist Sabina Rakcheyeva, Paris

Author with Sabina and her husband, Alec Haydon, New York City

Chapter 12

Where Did She Come From?
Where Is She Now?

Sometimes strange events, or very strange events, can pass through our lives with almost no notice. Sometimes it is only years later that we realize a mysterious event has been with us. Sometimes the event can be explained by extrinsic factors, but sometimes not—like a prime number, not divisible by anything. Then we are left with a perfect mystery, whole and complete in itself. But a mystery that is perhaps able to grow.

For many years I have been interested in piano music and often explore the more remote byways of piano literature. Eight years ago, I heard some charming pieces on the radio, composed by the nineteenth- and twentieth-century Cuban composer Ignacio Cervantes. I looked for a CD of his music, found several, and ordered one with performances by Juana Zayas.

While listening to this beautiful music, my mind began to wander, and soon I saw in my inner eye a middle-aged man wrapped in a yellow silk kimono and resting on an ornately carved bed. As I have a florid group of images and sounds passing through my mind most of the time, I didn't pay much heed to this vision.

But later that day I began to daydream about the scene and decided to write a historical fiction—a short story—about the

169

composer, Ignacio Cervantes, on the carved bed. In the story, he was thinking about his fifty-fifth birthday the next day and the big party that had been planned.

Marceline's tomb

As I began to write the story in my mind, a beautiful woman entered the daydream, coming in from Nacio's terrace. She was translucent, presumably a ghost or other spirit, and had come uninvited by me.

Who could it be? Where was she from? Why was she here? And what was her role in the story? As I gazed at her kind yet aristocratic demeanor, I could sense a name trying to enter visibility in my mind. The letters of the name became more distinct, as did her figure. The name became clear: Princess Marceline Czartoryska. Her name seemed unusual. The imagination can produce many surprises, but to pull these two names out of the air seemed unlikely, although I didn't really question the fact, accepting them as products of my imagination.

As I continued to compose the story, it seemed that Ignacio and the princess had been lovers in Paris many years before. I described the princess as the favorite pupil of Chopin and recipient of some of his manuscripts and wrote that the contemporary critics thought that of all Chopin's students, her playing was most like that of her teacher.

I told of the unusual love contracts that the princess drew up with some of her young lovers and also described her visit to the French ambassador at the court of King Mindon of Mandalay.

The princess was about to take over my story, as she became more interesting to me than the composer. But I pushed on, still trying to center the story on the composer. The fiction ended with Marceline and Nacio having a final, transworld physical ecstasy and then waiting for each other until death removed the final obstacle to their permanent union—a love story with a happy ending in death.

As I had always been at home with the ideas of life after death, and spirits of the dead had at times been part of my daily life, I saw nothing unusual about the ghostly aspects of the story except for its happy ending. But it turned out there was something definitely strange about the emergence of the story and its composition.

A few years after writing the story I went to Poland on vacation and of course visited the city of Krakow, where I was surprised to find that one of the outstanding tourist sights was the Leonardo da Vinci painting, "Lady with an Ermine," in the Czartoryska Palace. *What an odd coincidence of names*, I thought. On visiting the palace, in addition to the famed da Vinci, there were paintings of numerous Czartoryska family members, none of which were labeled "Marceline."

There was also a family tree drawn on a piece of parchment, which also contained no Marceline. *Oh well*, I thought. *That's the end of the coincidence. The name was just an odd imagination.*

Two or three years later, I was reading an article about the last days of Chopin and was astounded to read that on his deathbed, he was attended by four ladies, one of whom was his favorite student, Princess Marceline Czartoryska. So she had indeed existed! She had been born into the princely Polish Radziwill family, but upon marrying the prince, she had, of course, taken on his name.

The article went on to say she had received some of Chopin's manuscripts as gifts from him, and the critics commented that of all Chopin's students, her playing was most like that of her teacher, just as I had written. I had a slight shiver. How had I known so many obscure facts about her?

Who was this woman who was reaching out over the great divide? And why? I did some research and found that she was born Princess Marceline Radziwill, had been a star of European society, was known to Franz Liszt and other celebrities as well as to Chopin, and had had her portrait painted by Eugène Delacroix. In my imaginary story I assigned her the dates 1820 to 1882; in reality, they were 1817 to 1894.

But what had these facts to do with me? I loved Chopin's music, but that didn't seem enough to put me on such knowledgeable terms with his favorite pupil, now dead for more than a century. Perhaps my openness and hospitality to new (or forgotten) memories was enough to attract her attention.

For some time I had been thinking about the idea of orphan memories—memories belonging to real people now deceased or of events that are no longer remembered by any living person. These memories actually do continue to have a kind of independent existence, similar to the existence of ideas in a totally forgotten book—a book whose author died long ago and whose readers, although numerous in past times, have now altogether departed from this world. I didn't see much existential difference between an embodied memory (presumably living in someone's consciousness) and a disembodied memory (currently living in no one's awareness).

However, the disembodied, or orphan, memories yearn for a home. Related types of memories, such as memories of events that never happened, memories of events that will happen in the future, and memories of private, secret thoughts are all with us too—but perhaps better left to another occasion to write about.

How did I know these things about the princess, including her name? I believe I have become the home, for reasons unknown to me, to an orphan memory created by Princess Marceline. I have not, as of yet, found any evidence for her contracts with young lovers, including the two she made with Nacio. Nor have I found any verification of her time at the court of King Mindon in Mandalay. Perhaps in the annals of the French diplomatic service there might be some very discreet and oblique mentions of this royal and dangerous liaison.

Is this the end of the story? Or will further orphan memories from Princess Marceline continue to occupy more extensive territories in my mind? And how much more extensive? And to whom do they now belong? And after I die, in whose head will these memories reside? I welcome the adventure and perhaps can even hope for eventual contact with the princess.

New York, March 30, 2011

*Bhikkuni Miao Kwang Suddharma on the porch of her jungle cottage,
Anuradhapura, Sri Lanka.   Sister Miao reestablished the order of Buddhist
nuns in Sri Lanka after an absence of one thousand years.*

174

Snake charmer with his cobra, Sri Lanka

*Cage in hotel lobby, to protect the guests from aggressive monkeys,
Anuradhapura, Sri Lanka)*

Elephants at Kandy enjoying the water)

Taxi horses at Herrenchiemsee, Bavaria -- location of one of the grandest of King Ludwig's palaces

Hotel lobby, Budapest)

Public swimming pool Budapest

177

The Danube at Budapest, Buda on the far shore)

Front wall and gate, city of Lübeck

Partial view, wall and city of Avignon

Author in garden at Hong Kong

Steve, Ritz Hotel, Paris

Steve in garden at Hong Kong

Hong Kong

Carriages at Summerfest on Governor's Island, New York

Dog Valentine resting on the sofa, New York

Chapter 13

Birthdays

I had never attended a 100th birthday party before. The party was held at one of Houston's most pleasant clubs, the River Oaks Country Club, and was attended by a number of long-time Houston residents, most of whom were prominent Houstonians and had known each other for decades. My great aunt Mildred Japhet was the birthday girl and looked radiantly beautiful for this gala occasion.

Most of the party guests were family members. Mildred, or Mamie, as I called her, was the family matriarch and ruled over the family members like a benign empress. Both her beautiful daughters were at the party: Jane with her husband Gene Guinn, a cardiac surgeon called to Riyadh with Jane twice a year for a month at a time to take care of the Saudi royal family, and her other daughter Ann. Ann was present with her daughter Lynn and granddaughter Claire and Ann's husband Tom Cantwell, distinguished and brilliant head of several high-tech companies, later also to be president of my own family oil-field service company, Loomis International Inc., for which he did a spectacular job, including developing several new inventions useful in the drilling and related businesses.

Jane was present with her husband Gene, two handsome sons and the wife of her elder son, her daughter Gayle, a stunningly beautiful young woman with her husband, Lloyd Bentsen III, son of the outstanding Texas Senator, Lloyd Bentsen, Jr. who later was appointed Secretary of the Treasury. The Senator had been a few years ahead of me in the McAllen school system. We had been acquainted there, but were only casual school friends.

Lloyd III's brother Lan, a former US Congressman, and his wife Adele and daughters (one of them had very interesting Bette Davis eyes) attended the celebration, along with several of Aunt Mamie's old Houston friends, including the New Orleans and Houston resident, Gladys Thibodeaux, who owned sizeable plantations and who always decorated her Houston home lavishly and beautifully at Christmas. Mamie's neighbor Agnes was often present, sometimes accompanied by her glamorous friend, the retired Hollywood actress Gene Tierney, who always looked both melancholy and beautiful.

Many years before, Aunt Mamie had married Eric Japhet, one of three brothers whose father had discovered the world's largest oil and gas field, in partnership with Governor Hogg of Texas (father of the remarkably named Ima Hogg, a beautiful old lady and Houston philanthropist mainly responsible over the years for the outstanding Houston Symphony). This very valuable petroleum discovery had resulted in a financial bonanza for Mamie and her relatives, who now owned big banks, insurance companies, beautiful homes, large ranches, blocks of downtown Houston real estate with office buildings in place, and the other usual possessions and assets of the very rich. They had their own trust office downtown to help manage these holdings.

It was an era of innocent ostentation, when the rich could still enjoy their benign fantasies. One Houston man bought his wife a new Cadillac car for her birthday. When she remarked that it seemed a little dull, he had all the chrome removed, gold-plated, and reinstalled on the car. His wife thought it looked much improved. Another prominent oil man, affectionately called "Silver Dollar", liked to dress in red sequined cowboy costumes, and he was followed around by a very muscular young man carrying a large bucket of silver dollar coins. From time to time Silver Dollar would throw large handfuls of silver coins to the crowd wherever they might be, producing pleasurable consternation as many of the crowd scrambled to get the coins.

Some families built lakes in their back yards, large enough to have an island and need a motorboat to get about on the water.

184

Friendly competition thrived in that era. Several of Mamie's lady friends owned substantial parts of oil companies; one owned Chevron, another owned Texaco, another owned Exxon, some lived in huge apartments occupying whole floors of large hotels; another male friend had his own ballet company. That was Texas in that era.

Aunt Mamie's mother-in-law, charming and lovable, was a former opera singer and generous benefactor. Her husband had given her a major sparkler for her birthday, a diamond bracelet containing a number of very large stones. One day, when her three daughters-in-law were all together, they were admiring this spectacular piece of jewelry. She asked for pliers and a screwdriver and proceeded to operate on her bracelet, splitting it into three parts, each with several large diamonds; and then she gave a heavy piece to each of the girls, as equally divided as she could manage. Mamie had her diamonds reset in a beautiful ring, which she always wore and most everyone admired.

Once when Ann and Jane, Mamie's niece (and my aunt) Sadie, some other family members and neighbors were having cocktails in Mamie's living room, Sadie asked in her inimitable hoity-toity voice, "Mamie, do you think you will ever marry again?" There was an immediate increased attention in the room, perhaps partly because of the estate involved, and then Mamie said, "I will sleep with whomever I wish, but I will never marry again," and then she broke into a beautiful, gentle, and slightly mischievous smile, giving me an amused glance. I thought Ann and Jane and Sadie were going to fall out of their chairs. As they frowned and pretended to look disapproving, I added, "That's the spirit, Aunt Mamie, long life to you," as I tried to look benign and cheerful, and then gave her a thumbs-up.

At age ninety, Aunt Mamie was ramrod straight, with shining white hair, gleaming blue eyes, perfect skin, polished soft pink fingernails, and a lovely smile. She wore fashionable clothes, went to her beauty parlor weekly, and moved gracefully. She was kindly, charming, sophisticated, and very intelligent. In addition to all her virtues, she was open and sociable, with many friends, and she had a large fortune which she managed skillfully by herself. In other words, she was a catch. She even drove her own car until she was ninety-five, when too many slow collisions with pillars in the garage persuaded her to give up driving herself. Some of the more elderly Houston men were interested in her and asked her out, but she usually declined.

She had always enjoyed travelling. In her later years she had several times gone on safari to Africa, the last time at age ninety. One night, when she had needed to go out of her tent, she found an elephant standing outside. Fearlessly she advanced on the elephant, clapped her hands, and spoke firmly to the creature, which then scampered away, leaving Mamie in charge. The elephant was smart.

It was fascinating to me to see and visit with a family whose members seemed to love and cherish each other. I attended many family gatherings, birthday parties, weddings, dinner parties, trips to San Miguel Allende, weekends in Nuevo Laredo, barge trips in France, and other very pleasant excursions. Once when we were all in France, I asked Mamie's permission to purchase a gift for her, an outfit that she had been admiring from Chanel in Paris, but she declined with thanks. I settled for giving her a very attractive bright red cashmere sweater.

The family's social life revolved around Mamie's daughters, sons-in-law, brothers-in-law, grandchildren, other descendants, cousins, collaterals, and old friends.

Until about 1944, the family owned an estate on the north shore of Long Island. They often moved around in a large group, including going to the beach. In order to go to the beach together, they ordered a specially built Rolls Royce from the factory in England -- I gather it was something like a bus, in which twelve persons at a time could be transported. This odd Rolls and the north shore estate both came to an end about 1944, when the U.S. government confiscated the property to use as a convalescent home for wounded servicemen. I heard that eventually the government paid the Japhet family a fair price for the place, and so that was the end of the estate and the Rolls. But they had some others.

Mamie was aware that I did not have close family members around me and was mostly alone. She sometimes gave me advice and guidance, which I always valued. As she became older, she very slowly and most reluctantly had to curtail her social activities and mobility, rather resignedly settling for a cane, crutches, and eventually an occasional wheelchair, even somewhat moderating the high heels which she preferred. She would often look at me sweetly and say, "Do it while you can." I knew this was good advice, but it was only forty years later, when I too needed a cane, crutches, and an occasional wheelchair, that I realized Mamie was exactly on the mark (as usual).

She had enjoyed working behind the counter at the Thrift Shop of the Bluebird Circle, a charity devoted to bringing children's hospital rooms to one of Houston's leading hospitals. My friend Bill Berry once brought Mamie a fifty pound sack of rice for the Bluebird shop, and Mamie was very pleased. Once when I had an IRS audit, the auditor saw I had listed a contribution to the Bluebird Circle. He sneered, "Bluebird Circle. A likely story. I never heard of it," to which I replied, "This is a group of very prominent Houston ladies. If you tangle with the Bluebirds, you'll really be sorry." He closed his folder and went away.

My own family mostly related to each other in silence, usually with sullenness, secrecy, avoidance, and hostility punctuated by slightly more energetic angry periods. The family consisted of my father and mother, her mother, her two brothers and their wives. The family gatherings mostly consisted of occasional birthdays; we celebrated Christmas by ourselves. My mother was close to her mother and sister, otherwise members of the family were usually formally polite, but warmth and mutual support were not part of the relationships. When I see advertisements claiming that, "We treat you like family," my first inclination is to run the other way; certainly it is not an inviting comment.

So, being with Mamie and her family was like going into a different, better world, and I loved it. I saw what it was to have a happy marriage or valued relationships. Although I only saw this from the outside, I treasured the knowledge. It made me feel better to know and see that there was love and respect in the world. Maybe I too might eventually partake of this happiness.

But the years passed and birthdays accumulated. I thought that getting older meant bigger numbers on the birthday cakes, but otherwise all would stay the same. I wish I had understood earlier that this was not the complete story.

Mamie got more and more delicate. I continued to visit her when I was in Houston, sometimes visiting her alone or taking her out to one of our favorite Mexican restaurants. Once a waiter asked her, "Would you care for another drink?" She replied, "Yes, but this time put something in it!" She seemed to enjoy going out with me, and I certainly enjoyed going out with her. She continued to remind me to "Do it while you can," and sometimes gave me other good advice too. She began to stay in bed during my visits, and I started to sit on her bed while we talked -- that seemed more intimate and more cordial.

Her hundredth birthday came and was celebrated with a gala party. Then 101. Then 102.

One day she said to me, "If I had a son, I would want him to be just like you." My ears were dancing with joy.

I said, "I love you too. That's the dearest thing anyone has ever said to me."

"You belong to me," she said.

"Yes," I replied.

After a while, it was time for me to leave. "This is our last visit," she said, and I very sadly knew what she meant.

"Well, I will see you again. I promise," I said.

"You sure will!" she exclaimed with considerable force, almost a roar. She was 102 and had lived 1898-2000. She had lived in three centuries -- nineteenth, twentieth, and twenty-first   I gave her a kiss, murmured, "Goodbye," and reluctantly left.

And that was the end, for then, for now, but not for the future.

I was told that later that day her maid heard a tiny moan, and when she went into Mamie's room, she found that she had left this world.

She was buried in a shady corner of the cemetery next to Jane and Gene, Ann, and her husband Eric, who had been killed in an automobile accident on the same day that my father met the same fate. When I visit Houston, I usually visit the graves to say hello and bring each one a little flower. They all know.

Knowing Mamie was one of the highlights of my life. I believe I will see her again; she's expecting me.

Author at Houston Cemetery – burial place of Aunt Mamie and husband Eric, Ann Cantwell, Jane and Gene Guinn

Chapter 14

Twilight in Lübeck, 1673

Every summer from about 2000 to 2018, I attended a music festival, Rarities of Piano Music, held in Germany at the Schloss in Husum, a small town on the North Sea. Usually I started this trip in Hamburg, which had the closest international airport, often also visiting the nearby city of Lübeck. Once, while strolling on the Riverwalk in Lübeck, I noticed a row of grand houses. One of these houses particularly caught my eye. An eerie feeling of déjà vu took over my awareness: The house seemed totally familiar. Perhaps I had a connection to this house. In fact, I had the feeling that I had once lived there. This was the house of the Kaspari family.

Lübeck was the flagship of the Hanseatic League, the great mercantile association of the late Middle Ages and early Renaissance time. The league had somewhat protected the city, but even so, there was always anxiety about the future because of the widespread political and religious instability throughout Europe. The treaty of Lübeck had been signed in 1629, but that had not succeeded in bringing to an end the terrible conflict that came to be known as the Thirty Years' War. That had to wait until the Peace of Westphalia in 1648. By 1665 the populace of Lübeck was feeling secure again, and commerce was once again thriving.

Friday, September 15, 1673, was a sunny, warm day, the third and last of three successive perfect days. The residents of the town had already grown accustomed and indifferent to such days, for too many years of Hanseatic prosperity, power, and self-satisfaction had robbed them of the ability to appreciate and be grateful for such a small thing as a beautiful day. They had already forgotten the times of uncertainty and fear that had so recently come to an end, perhaps only temporarily.

Lübeck

The September air was very clear, but the slanting rays of the sun, due to the season and to the hour of four o'clock in the afternoon, were a harbinger of the autumn that was approaching. The flowers lining the Upper Riverwalk were at their maximum colorful late summer exuberance. The leaves on the chestnuts and oaks and birches were beginning to be frayed and bleached and tattered, although none of the lovely fall colors had yet appeared.

Occasionally, a chilly wind from the nearby Baltic would blow over the town.

The Riverwalk along the Upper Trave River was the most important street of the city. All the grandest houses were there, or close by, and the harbor was only a two-minute walk away. The ship owners, who lived in the grand houses, could be close to their businesses, and most of them enjoyed seeing their big merchant sailing vessels arrive, unload, reload, and depart again, each time bringing exotic cargo and the great profits that were the driving force behind all the activities in Lübeck.

The twin towers of the Marienkirche soared over the city, as if to proclaim the piety of the inhabitants. Although hypocrisy was widespread—then, just as there is now—there did exist an underlying current of genuine religious and powerful supernatural power, sometimes completely hidden, sometimes only thinly veiled. There were also strange stories and rituals that sometimes arrived aboard the sailing ships coming from distant parts of the world.

One of the grand houses on the Riverwalk was the Kaspari house. It rose five stories, topped by a steep roof and gables. Built in 1500, it was now almost two hundred years old. It had been in the Kaspari family since it was built and had been maintained in perfect condition. Horizontal rows of exactly aligned square windows gave an orderly pattern to the white façade. The house breathed an air of dignity, prosperity, safety, tranquility, and comfort. The hatreds, failures, betrayals, and miseries that had flourished there were not so readily apparent. Several generations of successful merchant-shippers had ensured that the Kasparis were financially secure. They were one of the richest families in Lübeck. A scene from the far past suddenly opened in my mind, and I seemed to be inside the house, witnessing long-ago activity.

The family was now smaller than usual, consisting only of the father, Karl; the mother, Johanna; and their three children, Astre, Genevieve, and little Maxie. Bonds of love and care united all five of them, with the exception of Astre, the oldest daughter, who was loved and who received the love, but sullenly gave back hostility.

The Kasparis were gathered in the master bedroom, the big front bedroom on the second floor. Weakening light was coming into the room through the bull's-eye windows with their yellow glass. The heavy maroon velvet draperies were partly closed, adding to the somberness of the scene. The dark wood paneling reflected very little light from the two flickering tapers. The massive wooden chairs, some upholstered in dark tapestry, were not inviting but had been pulled close to the bed and were occupied by the three children. Karl was sitting on the side of the large, high-canopied bed, gazing at his wife, Johanna, who was lying propped up on a pile of pillows.

She had been ill for the past year, suffering with a dull pain in her abdomen. This pain had grown gradually worse; she had lost her appetite, had lost weight, and felt weak and tired. In the last few days she had become much sicker. Johanna was looking at her family with eyes of love and sorrow. It was very quiet in the room. They all knew she was dying.

*****

Johanna thought back to her first meeting with Karl in 1641, when they were both children. She was four years old, he was six, and they were both out for a Sunday afternoon walk with their parents. While their parents chatted, the children looked at each other, smiled slightly, and then hit each other, and Johanna bit Karl on his forearm, making him yell. Their parents pulled them apart. That was the end of their first meeting but just the beginning of their relationship in this life. As the years went by, they occasionally saw each other.

To the surprise of everyone, especially Karl and Johanna, a strong attraction and an unchanging love began to grow between them. As their love grew, their spirits began to meet and grow together. As is sometimes the case with true lovers, when they were in each other's presence, they felt a comfort, a spaciousness, an understanding that didn't need words. They felt very well acquainted, much more so than could be accounted for by their brief years. They could feel each other's emotions, both happy and sad, even when they were not together. They knew it was their destiny to be united. And so it came to pass that they were married in 1657, when Karl was twenty-two and Johanna was twenty.

When Johanna saw Karl on their wedding day, she thought she had never seen anyone so handsome. He was six feet tall, had perfect erect posture and masculine bearing, and was very sturdily built with powerful shoulders and legs, delicate and sensitive hands of great strength, and a very handsome face. He had even features, shining teeth, an infectious smile and laugh, and dark hazel eyes that he used both to conceal and to reveal himself. He had magnificent dark brown hair, rich and lustrous, which when combed carefully gave an appearance of great elegance and vitality, but when left alone for a while, tended to revert to a more wild state and seemed to take on various arrangements almost as if it were alive.

He was generally cheerful and usually made those around him feel better, but he had occasional periods of sudden and unexplained extreme fear and hopelessness, which rarely lasted more than one or two days. He sometimes felt something wild and impulsive inside himself, which urged him to abrupt and overly forceful action; he had so far always been successful in suppressing this frightening tendency.

Geography and exploration fascinated him, and he wished he could have sailed with Columbus on his voyages of discovery almost two hundred years earlier. But at the same time, this idea filled him with dread—he thought it was probably just the excitement of the unknown that he was feeling, but sometimes he sensed a hidden subliminal memory from a long-past time. Occasionally one of these memories would suddenly light up, a picture of an unknown time and place, but would then close down again, remaining mysterious, but with hints of indistinct angelic presences.

He loved to dance, and he had a totally carefree side that he was careful to keep hidden. Without malicious intention, he could sometimes be thoughtless, selfish, and deeply hurtful to others; and then he was surprised at the results of his behavior. Karl was sometimes puzzled by visions of himself in unfamiliar or distant places, perhaps from another time, and sometimes with people he knew but did not recognize. He was a man of intense physical and sexual allure, of which he seemed or pretended to be unaware.

Karl, for his part, was overwhelmed with the gentle beauty of Johanna. She was of medium height, slender, and graceful. She had a full figure, which gave the impression of both strength and voluptuousness, an oblong face with a shy but intelligent expression, large blue eyes, a very straight nose, full pink lips, and light brown hair. She was very careful of her grooming and her appearance, and many thought she was quite lovely.

She had a musician's hands, rather larger than usual for someone of her size. She had played the harpsichord and the viola da gamba since childhood. By the time of her marriage, she was one of the best musicians in Lübeck. She was well educated and well read. Her moods were mercurial, usually cheerful, but sometimes melancholy and thoughtful, sometimes angry, and sometimes strikingly timid. But she was able to use her own emotional experiences and her sensitive intuition to help others when they were sick or suffering from spiritual pain, and it gave her much satisfaction when she could be of help.

Karl was the eldest of three sons. His two younger brothers were well-behaved boys, even if sometimes scheming, and they were the favorites of both parents. Karl was disliked by his father even more than by his mother, due to many episodes of thoughtless behavior, as well as a proud independence and an obstinate competence, and because he was resourceful and creative. Karl's father was jealous of Karl's physical strength and attractiveness and independence, and this eventually became an obsession. Some thought his jealousy bordered on the improper. Karl had sometimes worked for his father during holidays and had learned something of the shipping business, although he was not very interested.

His father, during one of his frequent bouts of heavy drinking, called Karl aside and said to him, "You have been indifferent to learning our family business, and you have taken no trouble to conceal your arrogance and distaste for me and for our family. I have decided that I do not want you to work in my business. When I die, which I expect will be many years away, of course, you will not inherit any part of the business or any of my other assets. I intend to take your two younger brothers into my firm and teach them the business, and they will eventually inherit it for themselves. My advice to you is that it would be best for you to leave Lübeck and seek your success elsewhere. You do not have my blessings on your life."

Karl was, of course, very disappointed by his father's words, but he was not surprised, as he knew that his father had never been his friend, even from his earliest days. If his family situation had been better, Karl would have preferred to stay in Lübeck and build houses, an occupation considerably less profitable and prestigious than shipping. However, as the family situation was full of hostility, he would have followed his father's advice to leave Lübeck if he had not been held captive there by his love for Johanna.

Johanna was the fourth of five children born to the Gartner family, having a younger brother, two older brothers, and an older sister. The boys were active, mischievous, and cheerful, while the two girls were both serious, studious, good musicians, kind, and considerate, but both had somewhat changeable moods. The children were all fond of one another and of their parents too. Their father, Manfred Gartner, was a successful merchant in Lübeck and was happy to use his money to try to make his family comfortable and happy, but he made the error of clearly favoring Johanna over his other children. He tried to hide his preference but was unable to consistently conceal it.

Their mother tried to make up for this by giving extra attention to her other four children, but the only result was that Johanna felt her mother preferred her other children and didn't like her very much. Johanna always wondered what she had done wrong to cause her mother to dislike her. She tried to win her mother's love by being very sweet, kind, and loving, but to no avail.

Because of this situation, which had lasted many years, Johanna was always afraid of being disliked by others for reasons she did not understand, and so she could not correct or compensate for whatever it was she might be doing wrong. She had always longed for someone she could absolutely trust not to suddenly turn against her, or to abandon her, and she knew that Karl was that perfect person for her.

And so on a brilliant spring day in 1657 the wedding of Johanna and Karl took place. It was a splendid occasion, as befitted the union of two of the most important families of Lübeck. Karl's parents, for the sake of appearances, feigned pride and happiness, and only a few knew their real feelings, which were disdain and animosity toward their son, along with a wish that the marriage would be unhappy. His brothers could hardly conceal their contempt for their brother and his bride. Johanna's parents were happy that their daughter was marrying a man she loved so much and who seemed to them such a good person, but they were worried for the financial future and security of the young couple, as they knew of Karl's father's plans to disinherit him.

As a wedding gift for public show, Karl's parents gave the young couple a small piece of land in Jamaica, which they had acquired through a foreclosure and which they had no interest to ever see or use. Johanna's parents gave them two fine horses, as well as a sum of money large enough to buy a good house in which to start their married life.

While they were making their plans as to their dwelling place and their future, they lived, as was the custom, with Karl's parents in the big house on the Riverwalk. This arrangement was very tense, with scarcely concealed irritation and animosity between Karl and his father and his two younger brothers. Karl's mother was a mild, weak woman who always took her husband's point of view, but she actually disliked Karl somewhat less than she pretended. She tried to get along with Johanna and actually enjoyed her company, after so many years in an exclusively male household.

One evening about six weeks after the wedding, Karl's father had far too much to drink and had a violent fight with a business competitor—a rival and enemy, whom he had unjustly accused of lying. He was badly beaten and was carried home, unable to walk, both from the beating and from his drunkenness. His family could see that he had been severely injured in the fight. He was put to bed in the big front bedroom on the second floor, which had been his and his wife's bedroom for many years, and the family tried to make him comfortable. He continued to mutter and shout drunken curses, and later that night, he gave a loud roar of hatred and pain and died, his mouth full of vile words he had not been able to utter.

All were sorry that his life had ended in such a miserable way. Karl and his mother were slightly saddened by his death. Johanna tried to comfort his widow and his two sons. The two sons were very distressed, as no will had been drawn. As was the custom, and in the absence of a will, the business passed to Karl, the eldest son.

When Karl understood the sudden change in his position, he decided that he and Johanna would stay on in the big family house on the Riverwalk. They moved into the big front bedroom on the second floor, and his mother moved to a smaller room on the third floor. Naturally, he permitted his mother to stay on in the house, and she was grateful to Karl and Johanna and ashamed of her previous behavior toward them.

He also invited his two brothers to continue living in the house until they finished their education, and they hated him for his kindness to them. They felt their drunken father had cheated them out of their expected inheritance and that Karl was somehow responsible.

When they finished their education, Karl offered them jobs working in his shipping business, but they both refused and showed increasingly hostile and sullen dispositions. Karl offered them each a generous sum of money to allow them to get started in a career or a small business, and then he asked them to leave his house. They accepted the money, they left the house, they cursed Karl and Johanna, and they left Lübeck. Karl never saw them or heard from them again. He occasionally learned something of their misadventures as they followed their father's path into drunkenness, evil temper, and violence.

Karl and Johanna began their married life blazingly in love with each other. After a few early cautious and delightful attempts, they found that they were more than compatible sexually. They loved the look, the taste, and the smell of each other's bodies. Johanna loved to smell Karl's fingers and she loved to gaze at the sides of his head. He, in turn, loved to touch her neck and shoulders and to bury his head in her bosom. When they were making love, their bodies seemed to fit together perfectly in all the many positions they discovered. For weeks they found it nearly impossible to take their eyes, their hands, their tongues, their mouths, their thoughts, and their feelings off each other.

Johanna loved taking Karl to a pinnacle of physical bliss in which he would lose all control of himself and would deliver his soul, as well as his body, into her hands. Karl was amazed that he could bring Johanna repeatedly to states of ecstasy, and he could feel her pleasure just as though he were in her body and soul, or as if their two souls could each feel the pleasure of the other. After a while, they realized that although their souls had fused long before they married, and that their bodies increasingly followed after their souls and also fused during ecstatic lovemaking, so did other parts of their natures fuse—playful, carnal, spiritual, gentle, ferocious, bestial, angelic, creative, demonic. In short, theirs was a complete union and fusion, the like of which is rarely encountered. Each saw the other as the most graceful, beautiful, handsome being imaginable; and when one of them spoke, the other heard the voice of an angel.

Their dispositions were perfectly matched and complemented each other. No energy was lost in arguing or struggling for domination. All their energies were used to build their lives together and to be in an almost constant state of joy. The townspeople thought they had never seen a happier or more radiant couple. Some, of course, were jealous and hated them for their happiness.

Two years after her husband's death, Karl's mother died peacefully in her sleep.

In 1659, just before Karl's mother died, Johanna gave birth to their first child, a daughter, whom they named Astrid. She was a beautiful child, blonde-haired and blue-eyed, but even as an infant she was fretful, irritable, and seemed to turn away from her parents. By the time she was four years old, she insisted on being called Astre and would scream with rage if anyone called her by her real name, Astrid. By the time she was thirteen, she had grown tall, cool, and beautiful.

She was aware of her appeal to and power over those who were attracted to her, particularly older men. She would be very pleasant to them, smiling and laughing, standing too close to them, touching their hands, and seducing their interest and lust, and would then suddenly turn cold and scornful. She enjoyed the consternation and pain she could cause this way. As the years went on, she developed this behavior until she could easily achieve a position of scornful, icy sexual domination over most men. She enjoyed hurting men and gained a reputation as a heartbreaker. She had scorn for all women too, but was not interested enough to make the effort to hurt them.

She knew that she had lying within herself a dead child—the innocent little girl she had never been—but she always kept this as her closest secret. After she was grown, she married a much older, very wealthy man, whom she treated with cruelty and who soon passed away, leaving her a large estate. Within a year, she had married another rich old man, with similar results. She then felt secure enough to spare herself the disgusting task of consorting with more revolting old fools. She was known widely as a haughty, cruel, and dangerous woman, and almost all were careful to treat her with caution and respect. She felt as if she were living inside a glacier, encased in ice, able to see out to the clear air and the sunshine but not able to free herself from her frozen coffin.

Two years later, in 1661, their second daughter, Genevieve, was born. She was also a beautiful child, thin and pale, and had her mother's auburn hair and hazel eyes. As time went on, she showed a high intelligence and a somewhat detached and observant manner, as if she were never quite a part of whatever was going on. She was generally cheerful, but sometimes exploded in rage, a trait that worried her parents. She had inherited her mother's musical interests, but her talent was exceptional, much greater than her mother's. She was friendly, and liked to play dolls with the other little girls of the neighborhood, but she would soon want to return to her music practice. For years, music was her primary interest; sometimes it seemed like her only interest.

When she grew up, Genevieve married a man who adored her, but for whom she had mixed fondness and contempt, perhaps more of the latter. She came to rely on his good will and protection, although she did not realize it, and of course never showed him any appreciation. She viewed herself as a misplaced princess and saw her husband as an uncouth lout, which opinions she did not try to disguise from her husband and her family.

In 1706, when she was forty-five years old, while on a visit to Leipzig, she played some of her own harpsichord compositions for Johann Sebastian Bach, who even at his young age of twenty-one was one of the most renowned musicians in all Europe. He was delighted with her performance and complimented her on her ability. They continued to visit each other occasionally and remained in correspondence for many years. Some suspected they were in love, in spite of the difference in age, and some even whispered (accurately) of a more carnal intimacy.

In 1665, four years after the birth of Genevieve, their last child, a son, was born. Political matters were still of great concern even at the time their child was born, and so they named him

Maximilian, after the two recent Holy Roman Emperors and after a recent ruler, the Elector and Duke of Bavaria.

Little Maxie grew up in a secure and generally happy household. His parents loved, protected, and nurtured him. Genevieve was fond of him and was very gentle and loving with him. Even Astre tolerated him without much animosity, although she could never be called warmhearted or friendly. Maxie was a strikingly handsome boy, with black hair, large dark eyes, and a most charming and disarming smile. He was extremely strong and could more than protect himself against the other boys in the neighborhood, and certainly against Genevieve and Astre if they tried to hit him or played too roughly with him. He was very independent and enjoyed wandering around Lübeck watching how people behaved.

While he was still a child, he was very protective of and helpful to his mother. He constantly thought of things he could do to make life more pleasant, happier, or easier for her. Even though he was very helpful to her, he was resistant to any suggestions or requests from her. He wanted his gifts to really be gifts, not filled orders. And he was highly critical, unappreciative, and rejecting of gifts others gave him—a trait that offended and hurt many people.

Later on, when he was almost grown, his father took Maxie into his shipping business. His intelligence, diligence, forcefulness, and good business judgment contributed greatly to their continuing success. His scrupulous honesty earned him a fine reputation and high status in the business community. Many, both women and men, were drawn to him because of his extremely handsome appearance, but that did not interest him. He wanted to be appreciated for his hard work, his competence, and the good things he did for others, not for something so superficial as his appearance.

Unfortunately, he did not learn to appreciate or accept gracefully what others did for him, gave him, or told him. Others came to understand that the only value they had for Maxie was to be recipients of his good works—and that he really was not interested in them as people. Relationships were truly one-sided: Good flowed from Maxie to others, but Maxie permitted nothing to flow from others to himself. Sycophants gathered; true friends did not. He felt a hollowness in his life.

And so the members of the family were gathered in the darkening bedchamber on the second floor, so familiar and such a reassuring sanctuary for so many years. They knew this was the last time they would all be together in this lifetime. On this September afternoon in 1673 Karl was age thirty-eight; Astre was fourteen; Genevieve, twelve; and Maxie was now eight years old. Johanna was thirty-six. Her illness was finally overcoming her strength to continue living.

She and Karl had had a final ecstasy of lovemaking the previous night—a night they would both long remember. Johanna knew that death was only a transition to another kind of life and that she would not lose contact with her family, but she was filled with sorrow that she could not continue to be physically present for her three dear children and for her beloved Karl.

She spoke to Astre. "Astre, my beautiful daughter, I have loved you every day since you were born to us. It troubles me greatly that you have been so unhappy and that you cannot take comfort and refuge in the love that surrounds you. Please promise me that you will try to develop the beauty of your soul so that it will match and then exceed the beauty of your physical being. This is the way to happiness for you. You have my blessing."

Astre replied, "I promise, Mother. Good-bye." Astre was serious but dry-eyed as they gave each other a final hug.

Johanna spoke to Genevieve. "Genevieve, my treasure, you have been a blessing from God to us. Remember that you have a great gift. You can reveal the divine to those who hear your music. You have a duty to bring joy and a glimpse of the divinity to many people. This may sometimes bring you the pain of sacrifice of your own happiness. But promise me that you will always share your music with others. You also have my blessing."

Genevieve replied, "I promise, Mother. Good-bye. I love you so much." Johanna and Genevieve both cried softly as they gave each other a very long and gentle farewell embrace.

The room had become darker. Johanna motioned to little Maxie to lie in the bed next to her. As she held him to her and stroked his hair and his face tenderly, she said, "Maxie, you have been like an angel to us. The kind and caring things you have done for me—the love you have shown me—have made me very happy and have made me feel safe. You are going to grow up to be a fine man—powerful, creative, and kind. You will bring happiness and comfort to many people. But you must learn to look with kindness and appreciation on the love and the ideas offered to you by others, as well as on their gifts to you. If you give to others, you must be willing to accept the gifts of others in return, or else your kindness will turn to poison. Please promise me you will try to accomplish this. You also have my blessing."

Maxie replied, "I promise, Mother. I want to give you happiness." As they embraced for the last time, no sounds came from their throats, but tears flowed from their eyes.

In the dark room, Johanna could see a movement in the air, and she became aware that five beings, their five guardian angels, were present, standing in the room, glowing softly, protecting, helping, and comforting them. The angels brought exquisite delicacy, infinite gentleness, and absolute safety into the room. They were eternal—time ceased to exist or to have meaning.

Her own guardian angel smiled lovingly at her, touched her gently on her head, and folded Johanna within her wings, easing her suffering. Johanna was aware that this feeling was familiar and recognized the angel had done this for her many times before. In fact, all through her lifetime she had been helped in this way. She and her angel looked lovingly at each other, and Johanna was flooded with a feeling of complete recognition and familiarity and with total trust.

Then Johanna turned toward Karl. They gazed at each other and into each other's eyes. They looked intently for a very long time. Their spirits fused more completely, more profoundly, more permanently than ever before. It seemed to them that they were one spirit inhabiting two bodies. They reaffirmed their union: Karl opened his body and spirit to future inhabitation by Johanna, and Johanna opened her spirit to future inhabitation by Karl. Then they pulled back slightly, and Johanna closed her eyes.

Karl kissed her on her lips. He could feel Johanna's spirit come into his body for a moment of bliss, and then she slowly drifted out again.

Karl whispered, "Please, Johanna, wait for me."

He could hear her whisper in farewell. "I'll wait for you forever, until we are together again. And I know you will be waiting for me too." Johanna knew that she and Karl were united for eternity, and so she serenely moved toward her transition.

A shimmer, a gleaming, a splendor appeared in one part of the room, and the golden angel of death appeared. She was more beautiful than Johanna could have imagined. She had light brown hair, large violet eyes, and the palest golden wings and was surrounded by the glowing colors of the sunrise. The other angels looked at her with eyes of radiant love. She was a spirit of immense kindness and reassurance. With her great love, she acted as midwife: skillfully and without any distress, she delivered Johanna's spirit from her body into the other world as her body took its last breath, and her family knew that she had moved into the next world. Johanna was astonished at the ease of her transition.

There was complete silence in the darkening room for the next two hours. Karl and the children barely moved as they lingered in the farewell. The room became almost completely dark, as night had fallen. They could feel Johanna gently brushing against them, and in their minds they could hear her whisper her loving good-byes.

The golden angel folded Johanna within her wings and gave her comfort and gave her some knowledge of her new condition. She helped her remember what she had known before. She allowed Johanna to see some of her previous lives, in which she and Karl had been together in many different relationships. Johanna saw and partially remembered these lives with love and gratitude, and she knew with certainty that she and Karl would continue to be together forever.

Johanna spoke to the angel. "I love my family very much. Please let me stay close by to help them. Please let me delay my permanent departure until the children grow up."

The golden angel answered her with a voice surrounding her like a soft cloud and said, "No, Johanna. It is for your own good that you must now begin your life in this new world. But because your request is made not out of selfishness, but out of love, you may return here on this date each year so long as any of your family is living." The angel kissed Johanna on her forehead and then put her into a profound sleep, from which she would eventually waken, completely rested and refreshed, understanding all the lessons of her past life and grateful for all her blessings.

Each year, on the anniversary of her death, Johanna's spirit, accompanied by her guardian angel, returned to the big house on the Riverwalk. Her family was always aware of her presence, and her spirit of love and peace filled the house and filled their hearts. Sometimes, as Karl was going to sleep, Johanna touched him on his face, and he was aware that she was present. As tears came into his eyes, he was filled with gratitude and love. Karl knew that Johanna was waiting for him, and he yearned for her. After forty more years passed, the golden angel returned and helped Karl to a blissful reunion with his beloved.

And so my memory of events which had transpired in the house where I may have once lived came to a gentle close.

Chronology

1618–1648: The Thirty Years' War
1629–May 29: Treaty of Lübeck signed
1635: Karl Kaspari born
1637: Johanna Gartner born
1648: Peace of Westphalia, end of the Thirty Years' War
1657: Karl and Johanna marry
1657: Karl's father dies
1659: Karl's mother dies
1659: Astrid (Astre) born
1661: Genevieve born
1665: Maximilian (Maxie) born
1673: Friday, September 15, Johanna dies, age thirty-six
1713: Karl dies, age seventy-eight

Chapter 15

The Slug and Lettuce, or the Snail in the Bathroom

Steve had been working in London for the past eight months and had a very comfortable two-bedroom apartment in the Spitalfields area, a few blocks from the Liverpool Street tube station, a major junction. It was on the second floor of a five-story town house, which had a rear entrance into a lovely gated and locked garden. It was a very convenient location, not too far from the City, the British Museum, Hyde Park, Piccadilly, and some prime shopping areas.

I had reestablished my previous schedule, spending about a month or six weeks in London and then a month or six weeks in New York. The flight between the two cities was only about six hours, much easier than the fourteen or fifteen hours between New York and Tokyo, and the jet lag also was not so severe. In addition to the fine museums, there was a rich musical life, and it was much more convenient to buy tickets in London than in either Tokyo or New York.

As part of getting settled in London, I rented an electronic piano and had it installed in the apartment. Music and piano playing had always been an important part of my life, both comforting and inspiring. Many years of lessons and practice had acquainted me with a wide variety of piano music. If I were not able to play the piano for an extended period, the sense of something important lacking in my life would become painful and somewhat disorganizing.

Over the years, technical improvements in the production of electronic pianos had resulted in a close facsimile of regular acoustic pianos, both in sound quality and keyboard and pedal action. The control of volume of sound produced and the ability to use earphones while playing made practicing/playing without tormenting the neighbors easy, even late at night or when quiet/silence was important. I was happy to be able to be reunited with my favorite composers—Chopin, Ludwig van Beethoven, Liszt, Franz Schubert, Bortkiewicz, Gabriel Fauré, and many others.

Author and Steve in London

Another aspect of my life that had to be reestablished was participation in Alcoholics Anonymous. London offered many meetings each week, and soon I discovered some meetings in convenient locations where I felt comfortable. I continued my long-time practice of attending several meetings each week, usually during the middle of the day. London, like New York, had several hundred meetings each week, including some that were primarily gay. The other members were welcoming to a newcomer, although not so warmly as in the Tokyo meetings. Regular attendance at the meetings helped to stabilize my life and emotions. I considered attendance at the meetings absolutely necessary to continue my sobriety and psychological comfort.

Steve at the Ritz Hotel, Madrid

So, I was then settled in several important ways in a new life in London. I found London a wonderful place to live, offering a wide variety of interesting and rewarding activities. The fact that I knew very few people besides Steve was no problem; my usual unsociable and solitary tendencies were helpful. When I would hear of someone being placed in solitary confinement, I always thought, *Well, doesn't that sound nice?* Apparently, I was lacking in ordinary human flocking inclination.

I also knew, in some way I didn't understand, that this was connected with the fact that I had never been bored. I was never lonely and never bored. These were two significant psychological/personal deficits that increased my comfort and self-confidence. I knew enough to try to keep these two traits hidden or disguised, as I had long ago learned that they often/usually aroused sullen hostility if I mentioned them.

Our long-time friend Douglas, who lived in Chicago, had recently lost his partner. We knew he was not pulling together very well five months after his loss.

Tower Bridge, London

I talked with Steve, who was working in London at the time and had a spacious apartment in the city. We both liked Douglas and thought it might help him to take a trip to London. We invited him to say with us. He accepted the invitation and soon arranged air reservations to come for a six-day visit.

Author in courtyard of the Victoria and Albert Museum)

Thursday morning I went to Heathrow Airport to meet Douglas, who arrived on the 6:30 a.m. flight from New York. He was the only passenger wearing a jacket and tie and seemed fresh and cheerful. We took the Heathrow Express to Paddington Station and then took a taxi to the apartment, arriving home about nine o'clock that morning.

*****

After unpacking, Douglas said he wanted to take a nap, and then we could go out for a while. After an hour and a half, he woke up, took a shower, and dressed, and we were ready to start out. I told him that a twenty-minute walk away was a cemetery where William Blake, Daniel Defoe, and John Bunyan were buried. His doctorate from Harvard was in English, and he was interested to see the graves of these famous writers. We walked over to the old Bunhill Burial Ground as it is called, and I showed him Blake's tombstone, which

211

had a little container of carnations in front, and also the grander monuments to Defoe and Bunyan.

He examined them carefully and then said, "What do you mean, saying they are buried here? The inscriptions say they are buried *near* here, but we don't know exactly where they are really buried, now do we?" He seemed cross and accusatory.

"Oh, I'm sorry. I guess I didn't look at the inscriptions closely enough. Shall we leave and walk home by a different route?"

"Okay," he said, not wasting any graciousness.

Later in the day, when it was time for dinner, we decided to find a local restaurant. I showed him all the local places. The new and stylish Canteen was too crowded. The Giraffe was a chain restaurant—no good. The Bangers and Mash was too common. The Scarlet was an Indian place—an ethnic restaurant, not acceptable.

Douglas said, "I *never* eat in ethnic restaurants. They are all cheap places, and their kitchens are filthy."

The Pizza Express was another chain restaurant—also not right. We were running out of places. The best hotel in the neighborhood, the Great Eastern, had three good dining places, but as it was already a quarter to eleven, they were all closing. I said I didn't know any other places in the neighborhood. We were in front of the grocery store, so I suggested that we might get some soup and eat at home.

Douglas was incensed. "I'm not just about to start cooking at this time of night. I want a salad!!"

"Well, maybe the Pizza Express might have something."

"Okay, if there's nothing better around here."

We went in and each ordered a salad, which arrived cold and crisp and was quite good. Douglas had two glasses of wine and seemed to relax a little. He asked me what the big building across the street was. I said it was an office building, but it had some shops and food places on its first floor.

"There is a Pret a Manger," I said and asked him if he knew what it was. "You can get—"

Douglas interrupted with a vehement retort. "Of course I haven't gone into such a place. I don't think you understand. I *never* go into fast-food places. I *hate* chain restaurants, although this salad is edible. I have never set foot in a Kentucky Fried Chicken, a

McDonald's, a Burger King, or any other similar pits, and I never will. It is important to me to have a decent meal in good surroundings. If I have to, I will cook it myself and use every pot and pan in the house to prepare something good for myself."

I was taken aback at this self-righteous and arrogant outburst. "That must take a lot of time. I envy your supply of leisure. I don't usually have the time to have two or three elaborate meals a day, and besides, it is too fattening."

"Nonsense. You don't have to eat everything that's set before you, you know. Use some self-control. I don't eat breakfast or lunch anyway."

Douglas had never had a weight problem.

"Yes, you're certainly right," I said, grinding my teeth in anger and impatience with this tedious exchange. We finished, went home, and both retired for the night.

*****

Not long after, we were sitting in the cocktail lounge of the Capitol Hotel, waiting for our dinner reservation. Douglas leaned forward conspiratorially. Smirking with self-satisfaction, he said in an enthusiastic whisper, "Cocktails are having a renaissance."

As someone who has not had a drink for twenty-nine years, I found this news somewhat underwhelming, but I wanted to make some suitably hoity-toity reply. "Oh, lovely," I said. "Perhaps standards are at last beginning to rise again."

The waiter appeared, asking if we would care for a drink before dinner. "A sidecar, straight up, of course," Douglas said.

Steve and I both asked for still water.

The sidecar and the water soon arrived. After saying "cheers" and clinking our glasses, we all took a sip.

Douglas said with a sneer, "This sidecar is no good. The bartender doesn't know how to make a decent drink."

We nodded gravely but said nothing—that was the prudent reaction to Douglas's comment.

*****

The next morning, Friday, I ground some good-quality coffee beans (Kenyan peaberry variety, from H. R. Higgins of Duke Street, royal warrant as coffee merchant to the queen) and made a pot of coffee.

Douglas rummaged around in the kitchen cabinets and then came out and said, "You don't have any proper cups and saucers, only mugs. I am *not* a mug person. I do *not* drink from mugs."

I went into the kitchen to check on what he had said and was surprised to find he was correct. I was ashamed to realize that I was a mug person. I had not previously realized I was a member of yet another group deserving of scorn. "Oh," I said. My self-esteem was taking a battering at Douglas's hands (or mouth).

Douglas said he was going out to look for a proper cup and saucer. About thirty minutes later he returned, bringing with him a small white mug and saucer. Apparently it had been the lack of a saucer that had disturbed him. He poured himself a cup of coffee and said, "Look at the color. It looks like weak tea." He took a sip and then said, "This coffee is no good. Throw it out."

Chagrined, I threw it out. I made a new pot of coffee, using about three times as many of Mr. Higgins's beans as the first time. Douglas took a sip. "This coffee is no good either. Throw it out," he commanded.

Meanwhile, I had poured myself a cup and found the coffee too strong for my taste, but otherwise okay.

"Don't you have any decent coffee around here? I suppose not. I'll have to get some good coffee when we go out today."

Later in the day he got a pound of espresso, which I found to be too bitter for my taste, but Douglas pronounced it to be just right. Over the next six days, he used about a quarter of the package, and when he left London he took it home with him.

That afternoon we went to the South Bank to the Tate Modern Gallery, where there was a big show of paintings by Henri Rousseau, paintings gathered from Europe, the United States, Asia, and England. I have always liked the fantastic, imaginative paintings of Rousseau and said I thought the show was interesting and charming.

Douglas said, "What a waste of time. What a bore. Second-rate paintings by a second-rate artist."

I didn't say any more about liking the show.

Before Douglas came to England, he had sent a list of restaurants he wanted to visit. These were all the most fashionable and expensive restaurants in London, and we went to some trouble to get the reservations. I like to visit a good restaurant occasionally, but every night for six nights was more than I liked. We hoped Douglas would enjoy this excess, but by the end of his visit, he hadn't said he liked any of the places.

That evening the reservation was at Gordon Ramsay's restaurant in Chelsea, which has three Michelin stars and was generally considered London's best restaurant. The only time they could give us was nine thirty, which was too late to suit me, although I didn't say anything about it, but the time was just fashionably right for Douglas. I was morose because of the ongoing verbal abuse from Douglas. Steve was tired but tried to put on a good front. Douglas had a few drinks, and a bottle of fine wine was ordered, so he seemed to get in a better mood and began to pontificate about other wines that he had had at various places in France.

Saturday morning passed sullenly, but with no outbursts or tirades from Douglas. He had bought three tickets for *Sleeping Beauty* at the English National Opera for Saturday afternoon, and Steve and I enjoyed the beautiful performance. Two young Russian girls were sitting just behind us, and they talked through most of the first act. Douglas said in a loud voice, "Be quiet! Be quiet!" but the girls continued chattering away.

They began taking flash pictures from their seats, which was strictly forbidden by the management. An usher came by to warn them to stop. In a few minutes they started taking more flash pictures. The usher appeared again and said in a moderately loud voice, "I warned you. Now give me the camera."

The girls did nothing, only giggled.

The usher said more sternly, "I said, give me the camera."

The girls giggled some more. Suddenly, Douglas turned around in his seat and roared at them. *"Give her the camera!"*

There was a ripple in the audience. The girls handed over the camera. I looked around at them, and they were scowling—obviously spoiled Russian pseudo-princesses.

After the performance, we took a taxi to the Capitol Hotel, another of the places Douglas had wanted to go for dinner.

He began a tirade. "I'm sick of people being so passive and leaving me holding the bag. I speak up to obnoxious people, like those Russian sluts, and then everyone leaves me holding the bag. Passivity makes me sick." And so on.

I smiled a little, thinking that the only way anyone could get on with this old fart was to say nothing "passively" and let him rant on "actively."

Until that point, I had thought of the situation as a visit from an old friend who was troubled, but I still hoped we could have a good time together and remain cordial. In the taxi, I realized that the true situation was that Douglas would continue to throw buckets of filth, no matter what I said or did, and that I should just duck my head, clench my teeth, and try to wait out this nasty visitation. I began to think of him as a surly curmudgeon who would be best avoided in the future. But I wanted to keep my self-control and not to blow up at my guest.

Reaching the Capitol Hotel bar, we then heard more about the renaissance of the cocktail. *Blah, hot air, blah, blah.* Seated at the table, enjoying an excellent dinner (with plenty of wine), the talk turned to travel. Douglas wondered where he might go next.

"Have you been to Brazil?' I asked.

"No. *All* Brazilians are shallow, exhibitionistic, and loud. I would never go there—or anywhere else in South America, for that matter."

"I suppose that's wise," I said passively. But I thought, *Why don't you shut up, you bigoted know-nothing? You're just a piss-elegant pretentious old queen. A mean one, at that.*

The conversation came to a halt for a while. Then we finished dinner and went home. Douglas seemed oblivious to the nasty effect he was having. At home later that evening Steve told me (privately) that Douglas was the most insulting, negative, prissy, and pretentious person he had ever known. He said he hadn't seen a queen like Douglas for a long time.

The next day, Sunday, was quieter. Steve was home all day, which perhaps slightly inhibited Douglas's impulse to be nasty. Steve had gone out early to the bakery to get a loaf of freshly baked bread. Back in the kitchen, he sliced off a few pieces to make toast for breakfast.

Douglas said, "Why are you ruining fresh bread by toasting it? Do you always do that? Do you like to ruin it?"

Steve didn't give any response.

Douglas went out for a while in the afternoon. He planned to visit the British Museum. He did not invite us to go with him, and we did not invite ourselves.

That evening we had dinner at the Ivy, another old luxury spot that had excellent food. Douglas was disappointed that they did not have a special roast chicken dish he had read about. It was on the menu but had sold out already. Douglas made a to-do with the waiter, saying he had come four thousand miles and couldn't they provide just one more?

"Sorry, no." he said. The waiter was pleasant, but I wondered what he was thinking.

The dinner passed without too much argumentation or pretentious queen commentary, but I was glad to get home afterward.

The next day, Douglas wanted to have lunch at Wilton's, a fine seafood restaurant on Jermyn Street. They had a table available, so we enjoyed a very good lunch. Douglas told me in the middle of the lunch, "I saw a snail in your bathroom last night. Do you want me to kill it? I suppose you're too passive to do the job yourself."

"Oh well," I replied. Afterward, I went home, and Douglas went shopping.

That evening we had tickets to hear the French pianist Pascal Rogé play an all-Debussy recital at Queen Elizabeth Hall in the Southbank Center across the Thames. The concert was beautiful. Douglas had not eaten, so after the concert he suggested we go to the Pizza Express so he could have a salad again. I had an impulse to tease him about going to a chain restaurant but thought better of it. He made no comment on the concert or the meal.

Tuesday was his last full day in London, thank God. In the morning, after he had had his own special coffee in his own special cup, he said he was going out for the day. "Oh," I said. He didn't say where he was going or ask if I would like to come along. I was delighted at this arrangement.

We had a reservation, which had been especially hard to come by, that evening at seven thirty at Tom Aikens. Steve would meet us there, coming straight from his office. According to Douglas, this was the hottest restaurant in town, and Tom Aikens was the hottest chef in town. I hoped we wouldn't be incinerated. Before he left for the day, Douglas asked how long it might take to get to Tom Aikens. I said we should allow an hour. He went out without saying good-bye.

That evening, I was ready to leave for Tom Aikens by six thirty, an hour before the reservation. Douglas said it was too early and that I had said thirty minutes would be enough time.

"Oh, no, I didn't. I said we should plan for an hour."

He glared at me. I looked in the London restaurant guide and wrote down the address and telephone number of Tom Aikens. He was a little agitated that he had left my house keys at Harrod's Cafe but insisted on going back to Harrod's to retrieve them. Douglas puttered around for another thirty minutes, and then we departed. I suggested we take a taxi, as we were now going to be late, but he didn't want to. So we headed on foot for Liverpool Street Station and the tube.

As we were walking to the station, Douglas began again. "The restaurant guides are so cheap and pretentious. They are always talking about how expensive such-and-such restaurant is. All they are interested in is the price of the meal—the higher the better. How coarse! They are just fakes. They don't care anything about the food. The people who read the guides can't afford to go to the restaurants anyway. And they write it for stupid, coarse Americans who don't know anything, people who want to be told what is good and where they should go."

Irritated, I tried to make a reasonable reply. "I find it handy to have a list of the restaurants with their addresses and telephone numbers."

Douglas retorted, "I read the restaurant reviews in the *New York Times*, the *Financial Times*, and the *Wall Street Journal*, and I remember what the reviews say. So I don't need any listing of names and addresses. I keep them in my head."

I didn't believe what he said but didn't care to argue with him. When we got out of the South Kensington tube station, close to Tom Aikens, we were already five minutes late for our reservation, and Douglas began to get frantic. "Let's take a taxi," he said and began to rush up the street waving his arms. There were no empty taxis. But then one stopped right in front of us, and the passenger got out. We jumped in, and Douglas yelled at the driver to take us to Tom Aikens's restaurant.

"What's that?" the driver said. "I don't know where that is."

It was fortunate I had written the address down, so we could tell the driver the address we wanted. It was only a couple of blocks away, but because of the one-way streets and the rush-hour traffic jams, it took us almost thirty minutes to get to the restaurant. Steve was waiting impatiently (he is almost never late for an appointment). The restaurant was still holding our table.

When we looked at the menu, we noted that it listed several ingredients unknown to us, and we began to talk about all the unusual ingredients that were available almost worldwide in these days of jet transport.

I began to tell a story I thought was amusing. "Once Steve and I were having lunch in the Spring Moon restaurant at the Peninsula Hotel in Hong Kong, a very nice place. When the—"[1]

---

*This is the story I wanted tell: Several dishes were served, all delicious. Sometimes it was hard to tell what the basic food item was, due to the dicing techniques and the unusual spices.

JL to waiter: "What is this delicious dish?"

Waiter: "Cat meat, sir."

Thinking I had misunderstood, I repeated: "What is this delicious dish?"

Waiter: "Cat meat, sir."

Steve, just tuning in: "What did he say?

JL: "You don't want to know." Douglas would have fainted if he had heard.

Lucky for him that he had cut off the conversation earlier. Steve and I had a good laugh. I never did decipher what the waiter was trying to say. I hoped the dish was not cat meat.

Douglas broke in with a stern comment in a loud voice. "That's a Chinese restaurant. What would you expect? They serve out any kind of crap, even cat meat; you can't tell what it is. They make you sick. They are all cheap places, and their kitchens are filthy. I would never eat in such a place." He was repeating himself. He looked smug and was obviously pleased to have thrown another insult. The fact that he was talking about a very fine restaurant, and one he had never visited, didn't cause any prudence in his talk. In other words, he didn't know what he was talking about.

Steve was aware of what had happened and tried to save the occasion. "Well, John, please finish your story." He smiled at me.

"I don't care to speak further of the matter," I said with as much huffiness as I could manage. In fact, I didn't say a word for the next hour. Then I excused myself to go to the men's room. While I was away, Steve told me that Douglas said to him, "Well, you really have your hands full, don't you?"

The food was good, but I wasn't able to enjoy the meal. Douglas seemed to relish his dinner and especially his drinks, getting more pontifical and insulting as the evening progressed. Perhaps retrogressed would be a better word for what was happening.

The next morning we were all up early. Douglas had packed the night before. He left early to go to Harrod's to retrieve the keys. Two hours later he returned, keys in hand.

"Thank you," I said.

It was time for him to leave for the airport, and I helped him to get to the taxi corner. "Good-bye. Good-bye," I said. "Thank you for coming to visit us."

"And thank you for having invited me." He got into the taxi and was off to Paddington Station to catch the Heathrow Express.

Two days later, he sent a polite e-mail thanking us for our hospitality. I responded that I was glad to hear he had reached home safely. There was no talk on either side about any further contact.

*****

That evening Steve said, "The snail is in the bathroom." I went to see, and there it was—about the size of the last joint of my little finger, dark gray with a pointed back end and a rounded front.

Coming from its head end were two little waggling stalks, which I took to be its eyes. As it had no shell, I guess technically it was a slug. It was charming. We named him Sluggy. His picture is included here.

This benign little being glided serenely along on a low outcropping of the bathroom wall. I put down some small celery leaves close to it, and it changed its course toward the greenery. Another evening I saw it sliding toward the celery, waggling its eyes. I thought it was enthusiastic about having dinner. Another time I saw it just as it reached the celery. Its eyes were moving about happily. It was obvious to me that Sluggy was in a jolly mood. I took a picture of him looking at the celery leaves. We never discovered where he stayed during the day. Once I went into the bathroom and called, "Sluggy! Sluggy!" And Sluggy came sliding out on top of the tub, a coincidence, I am sure. I was so glad that I hadn't let Douglas kill it, bloodthirsty snail-murderer that he is.

His self-esteem seemed to depend on maintaining an image of himself as a person of exquisite refinement and good taste. This, in turn, depended on his observing an elaborate and idiosyncratic code of dining trivialities, which seemed to govern his life, perhaps made up on the spot to offend someone present. No opinion other than his was to be tolerated. He had become a thorough bully. Never did he seem to have any sense that he was not behaving well, that he was being rude and inappropriate, or that he was being hurtful and giving offense. Perhaps he was the Emperor Nero in his previous life.

It was humiliating and tiring to continually pretend that nasty personal insults had passed unnoticed.

I needed several days of rest and seclusion after Douglas left.

*****

A week later I had the roll of photographs developed, including some of Douglas's visit. There he was: well-dressed, with a handkerchief in his coat pocket, slightly crouching, as if to spring to the attack. He glared at the camera with his chin thrust forward and his mouth twisted into a snarl. Seeing him gave me a shudder. I saved one of his pictures as a souvenir, a warning to myself. I threw the rest of his photos into the garbage. This putrefaction of the relationship was quite shocking to me.

221

I had also taken a picture of Sluggy looking at his celery leaves, and this was very dear. I thought it was unusual to meet a snail with a better personality than a human person. This was the silver lining to this experience.

As the Buddhists say, "May he have happiness and all causes for happiness. May he have relief from suffering and all causes for suffering." (And me too.)

I hope I never hear from him again. As of two years later, my wish was coming true.

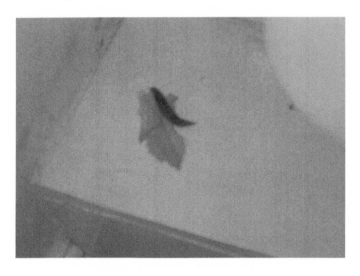

Portrait of Sluggy with a celery leaf

Chapter 16

Jerusalem

There is a pair of conflicting inclinations in my psyche. One is an inclination to stay home, safe and cossetted in my cozy snuggery. I love my little apartment home in the sky in the middle of Manhattan, the spacious terraces filled with plants carefully tended over many years, the interior cluttered with books and CDs, Tibetan bronzes and paintings, with the huge Steinway concert grand piano at one end of the living room, hulking like a black bull with eighty-eight shining white teeth guarding me and the premises and my problems, but always ready to sing sweet songs to make my life easier and more beautiful. This piano was for many years the Steinway instrument used at the music hall in Houston when visiting artists were giving programs, and I have heard my piao played in recitals by many of the leading artists of the day, including Artur Rubinstein, Myra Hess, Vladimir Horowitz, William Kapell, Vladimir Ashkenazy, Rudolph Serkin, and many others, so I know what it can do. I sometimes laugh and say, "My piano already knows how to play very well, much better than I do."

We enjoy fourteen foot ceilings in the apartment and large windows looking onto the terraces. I am also on the best of terms with my bed, which stands in my green silk-lined bedroom, also sheltering my sweet little dog friend, Dixie. I have lived here for fifty-six years, a very long time by New York standards. Most of the people I have loved have been here for times varying from a few hours to many years. The apartment is home to numerous revenants and shadow people (there is even an occasional perfume ghost, who has been with me since we first met at my house in Ridgefield, Connecticut thirty years ago), so the place is sometimes full of knockings, squeaks, rattles, fragrances, and other hellos; perhaps there are occasional soft, almost inaudible whispers and sighs and the most gentle touches, like the end of the exhalation of a sigh or the final sounds of a mother's song. These sounds keep me company and do not frighten me. There have been many happy events here and almost as many sad ones, and I can see them all when I look carefully, and I can sometimes carefully revisit them. I spend a good deal of time sitting at my desk, tending to paper work, reading, musing, using the computer, playing the piano, and talking on the telephone.

About five years ago I began to have difficulty playing the piano. There was no pain, no pronounced weakness or lack of coordination. Recently I described it as being impotent in the hands, or running on empty fingers. I have consulted numerous and varied physicians. They have all done careful examinations and ordered numerous tests. One neurologist recently ordered $9,000 worth of spine x-rays, fortunately all reimbursed by the US insurance program, Medicare. Aside from arthritis under my right kneecap, nothing has been found. The doctors say, "We cannot find anything wrong with you." Then I say, "Yes, but I still can't play the piano; my fingers just don't move right," and the doctors reply "Oh, yes."

The doctor visits were not without risk: one neurologist wanted me to do such a strenuous test of my legs (standing on my toes on one foot), that one leg was damaged, was quite painful, and took three months to mostly heal from his totally useless and unnecessary procedure. It was as if an eighty-four year old patient previously unknown to an internist consulted the doctor complaining of chest pain and shortness of breath, and then the doctor said, "I want you to run around the block three times, as fast as you can go, so we can check your cardiac reserve." As the patient was running around the first block, he fell over dead. The good doctor then said,

"I guess his cardiac reserve wasn't good, but now we know this valuable piece of information. The bill will be $9,000."

But even without a diagnosis I still had an increasingly severe piano problem. I could now play a maximum of two pages, and then my hands would be tired out. Lately my balance also began to be unreliable, but at least I (probably) do not have any of the very severe neurological disorders, such as multiple sclerosis, Parkinson's disease, muscular dystrophy, amyotrophic lateral sclerosis, and wasting diseases of muscles, all of which tend to progress and none of which are curable at present. So at this time my disorder is not guaranteed to progress or even to remain as it is now, but perhaps it will become less mysterious (and perhaps more treatable.) I have said, "nothing works quite right, but nothing hurts."

But I recall Aunt Mamie's mantra, "Do it while you can," so last year I began to think of places I would like to visit while I can, and chief on the list was a visit to Israel.

Several years ago, my mother and I had twice planned a visit to Israel, and later Steve and I had also planned a visit. All three times war, or at least serious hostilities, broke out in the vicinity, and so the trips to Israel had to be cancelled.

But the situation had been generally quiet in the Middle East lately, so we decided to try again, this time going to Germany to the Husum festival as usual in August, then on to Israel, and finally back to New York. After reading guide books to Israel and noting the very large number of historical and religious sites there, and how close they are together, we decided to go directly to Jerusalem and make it our base for further explorations inside Israel. Considering that the whole country is not very large, we could make round trips from Jerusalem to almost any location in Israel in one day, and we preferred not to have to keep moving hotels and wasting a day in packing and transit each time. We also considered going to Petra in Jordan, but read that considerable walking was necessary; also crossing a hostile border, so we decided to restrict ourselves to Israel.

The trip to Husum was a delight, as usual. After the piano festival, which lasted eight days, we drove to France, passing close to the French Riviera with its famous and deluxe resorts. We passed close to the resorts and then close to the medieval walled city of Carcassonne, where we spent two nights in a fine hotel, exploring the

225

ancient city, which appeared so strange and other-worldly it seemed to be enchanted, magically rising up from the past. I found the atmosphere somewhat sinister, as though the whole scene might suddenly disappear back into another dimension, carrying me along like a piece of baggage.

The night before boarding the four hour El Al non-stop flight to Tel Aviv, we spent the night at the airport hotel, re-emerging for a while into the modern era.

The plane flew south as far as the Mediterranean and then turned east heading for Israel. We passed over many islands, some quite large (perhaps Cyprus or Lesbos). As we crossed into Israeli airspace, I could look down on the Holy Land and was aware of a strong feeling of awe, knowing the tremendous events which had transpired there.

The Tel Aviv airport is between Tel Aviv and Jerusalem, somewhat closer to Tel Aviv. We had reserved a car with driver to take us to Jerusalem. We drove through the arid scenery, punctuated by new modern settlements and occasional small towns. After the one hour drive to Jerusalem on a very good, smooth road through a maze of walls and fences, some with flaring tops to guard against rocks thrown by angry Palestinian youths, we could see the old city of Jerusalem in the distance, with the prominent Dome of the Rock in the middle of the scene. We could also see the Western Wall, sometimes called the Wailing Wall, which had been built by King Solomon as one of the walls of his great temple. The walls of the old city were all in tones of light brown and gray, very beautiful in a somber, dignified, and restrained palette. The high outer walls were pierced by a number of major gates, which appeared to be nodes of activity. In one location there was a huge cemetery at the base of the wall.

We drove directly to our hotel, the King David, a large and elegant seven-storied structure more or less in the middle of the old city, sitting on top of a sizeable hill. (The arrangement and luxurious style of the King David reminded me very much of the wonderful Mamounia Hotel in Marrakech, Morocco.) As we went along on the excellent road, I noticed many features similar to those at home: sidewalks and curbs, street lights and traffic lights, crowds of people walking along just as in New York, but also an occasional camel. I was very much aware that although many features of the place seemed familiar, I was in a truly remarkable and unique place, and a small thrill ran up my spine. I felt I could somehow sense the truly special and otherworldly atmosphere, and I thought of the religious significance of the places we were passing; also echoes of the long and fantastic history that was all around us.

We drove up to the front door of the hotel, attendants took the car away, and we were shown to our rooms. We passed by the large lobby filled with cheerful sounding people, and I noticed the coffered ceilings, all elaborately painted in rather muted but lovely colors, and several expensive looking shops whose windows displayed fine luxury products. This was a very elegant and affluent scene. Jerusalem was an expensive city to visit, prices were about 10% more than in New York.

From our rooms, we could look out to other hills some distance away. The landscape was dotted by palm trees. The old city covered several hills and could not be completely seen from our rooms, but was marked by a number of minarets, domes, towers with pointed tops, and some five and ten story buildings. Before dinner we went out for a short walk in the vicinity of the hotel. As it was just about sundown, it was starting to get cool. The temperature was about ninety degrees at midday and about fifty degrees at night, a typical spread of temperatures in this desert climate; hot in the middle of the day, with bright sunshine, and slightly chilly in the night, enough to require sweaters or coats. There was very rarely any rain. In the distance large hills and higher mountains with snowy tops were visible. The Mediterranean was about twenty miles to the west.

There were adequate sidewalks, but the entire ground was covered by paving stones and rock and tile sections. Nowhere was really smooth, and the ground was irregular enough to make maneuvering a wheel chair somewhat bumpy. The unevenness of the ground made it slightly difficult for me to walk, even when using my cane and being careful.

Reading the guide books was impressive. There was a sight every few feet. Here Abraham baked a loaf of bread -- there Sarah had a vision of an angel, and over there the miracle of the loaves and the fishes took place; King Solomon had had a dalliance over there;

227

here is the place where Jesus cured the lepers. I had never been anywhere with such a concentration of really famous, mostly religious, monuments, or places/events described in the Bible or in other ancient texts. Many of the events were in the locations where Jesus or the Virgin Mary had manifested, and many events memorialized had happened prior to the birth of Jesus, as Jerusalem was a very ancient city.

Our driver, a former member of the Israeli armed forces, was big, strong, handsome, and carried a gun -- this was our first close-up encounter with the tensions of this location. He was very polite, well-spoken, and was an excellent driver. He was with us all day every day while we were in Israel, and his presence was reassuring as he drove us about in a large SUV, sometimes attracting curious looks from passers-by. We also had a full-time guide who was with us at all times when we were out of our hotel. She was a very attractive young woman from Estonia, who had grown up in America, but had been living in Israel for twenty years. She was very pleasant, well educated, and was an expert on Israeli history and culture, and was enthusiastic about what we were seeing on our tours.

We spent most of every day touring or visiting fascinating sights in Jerusalem. Due to the winding streets, the hills, and the general antiquity of the buildings, I was never really oriented as to where we were, but most of the places we visited were inside the walls of the old city.

As it was midsummer and with no major religious holiday pending, the crowds were small; we did not have to wait in lines to enter any of the places we visited.

One of the first places we saw was the Church of the Annunciation, in Nazareth, where the angel announced to Mary that she was to bear a divine child. Later we went to the Church of the Holy Sepulcher, a larger structure in the old city of Jerusalem. It is administered under the jurisdiction of several religious groups, with a fair degree of cooperation. Here is Golgotha, where we stood on the very place of the crucifixion. There was a strange, hushed atmosphere. We went on to Jesus's tomb, a small, low ceilinged room at one side of the church, where his body was kept for a short while after the crucifixion. I was in a wheel chair, but Steve was able to push me into the tomb, where I just fit under the ceiling. The other pilgrims/visitors gave me a curious but mild glance, and I soon went on my way. Because of the wheel chair, we decided to skip the Via Dolorosa and the Stations of the Cross (all were clearly marked). Perhaps we could visit it later.

Outside the Church was the Mount of Olives and the Garden of Gethsemane. I was very moved to be in these ancient holy places which I had heard of all my life. There is a very powerful atmosphere of solemn sanctity.

Higher up on the Mount of Olives is the Church of St. Mary Magdalen, somewhat off the usual tourist route, which I had specially wanted to visit. I had been interested for years in the Romanov family and their tragic fate. One of the final imperial Romanovs was the Grand Duchess Elizabeth of Russia, known in the family as Ella, sister of the last Empress, Alexandra, slaughtered at Ekaterinburg. At a nearby place, Ella, who was often described as the most beautiful princess in Europe, was clubbed on the head and then, with several other family members, thrown down a mine shaft while she was still alive. Finally, flaming liquid was thrown down on the poor unfortunates. A saintly person, Ella tried to help the other victims by using her clothes as bandages, but all of them perished painfully by starvation and injuries. Ella had done many good works. She was canonized by the Russian Orthodox church and is now usually referred to as Saint Ella Romanov.

She was entombed in this church, as was her niece, born Princess Alice of Battenburg. After Alice's marriage she was known as Princess Andrew of Greece, mother of Prince Philip of England, consort of Queen Elizabeth. Princess Alice's coffin was draped with the royal flag of England. One floor above Princess Alice's coffin was Grand Duchess Ella's tomb. Ella's coffin stood by itself in a sizeable chapel. I was surprised to see that the sides and top of her coffin were glass, and Saint Ella's body was visible inside. She was clothed in a long dress of somber gray and floral brocade. Her little embroidered shoes were visible at the bottom of this dress. Her face was completely covered by another piece of beautiful brocade held in place by a coronet-like apparatus. Her companion, Sister Varvara (also Russian) lay in another coffin nearby. The whole impression was lovely, quiet, dignified, and sad.

After remaining quietly in the chapel for fifteen minutes, we silently left and went out onto the portico of the church. The brilliant sunlight was blinding, and the dark upright cypresses exactly matched the mood and atmosphere of the location. From the side of the Mount of Olives, we could look out over the rest of the church grounds and over the city of Jerusalem. We strolled for a while in the Garden of Gethsemane, which still exists as a quiet haven.

Our next stop was the Western Wall, sometimes called the "Wailing Wall). This giant construction, about one hundred feet high, was a wall of King Solomon's temple, and is very well preserved. The plaza next to the wall was almost completely filled with praying Jewish men, mostly in long frock coats, with beards and wearing large fur hats. They bobbed backward and forward in their devout rituals, and one of them offered to show us the correct procedure for praying at this holy shrine. We were very moved.

A little higher up the Mount of Olives was the Temple Mount, with the Dome of the Rock on the summit. This is a very holy Muslim shrine and is not open to non-Muslims.

The next day we drove to the Sea of Galilee, a very beautiful body of water, with many cypresses. Just across the Sea was Jordan, and the Golan heights were in plain view. We had a pleasant lunch here, looking over the Sea of Galilee.

The following day we drove south for about an hour to visit the Dead Sea. There are a number of luxury hotels on the beach, and they welcome day visitors. The Dead Sea water, said to be therapeutic, can be enjoyed at the beach or in large swimming pools maintained by the hotels. We checked in to one of the pools, changed clothes in the locker room, and then went into one of the pools. It was a novel sensation to try to get into the pool, due to the very high salt content of the water. The water almost seemed elastic; it was like trying to get into a bowl of pudding. (I remembered years ago visiting the mud baths of Dr. Wilkinson in Calistoga -- the mud was said to be therapeutic. After taking off all our clothes, we sat down on the mud. I was surprised that it was not at all soft -- it was like sitting naked in the garden, and then tying to wiggle down into the soil.) After paddling about in one of the Dead Sea swimming pools for a while, we showered, changed clothes, and left. An odd experience.

We went on to the fantastic fortress of Masada, built atop a mountain as a place for a last stand against invaders. Fortunately there is an elevator, as the cliff is two thousand feet high. Then we returned to Jerusalem and had our last dinner across the street on the open terrace of the Ritz-Carlton Hotel.

Generally the food in Israel was good, mild, wholesome, but constrained by the dietary laws, which forbid mixing meat and dairy products in the same meal (or in the same kitchen). The next day we left for the twelve hour non-stop flight from Tel Aviv to New York.

The trip to Israel was much more interesting than I had anticipated. For any of us who had grown up in the West, I think that Israel is part of our heritage, no matter whether we be Christian, Jewish, or Moslem. To get a real feeling of our ancient heritage, I would recommend visits to Istanbul, Athens, Rome, Egypt and the Nile, Morocco, and of course Israel and most of Europe.

I personally felt strangely at home in all these places, and the experiences were not easily captured in words.

Chapter 17

Lourdes

Two years later, my playing had become even more uncertain and difficult. I was unsteady at the piano and sometimes had to rest before the end of the composition. I had fallen several times, but fortunately had not been injured. Falls sometimes led on to the demise of the elderly (I was eighty-two.) My maximum time playing was limited to between thirty minutes and one hour; which was inadequate to make any real progress at the keyboard. There was no pain or discomfort or paralysis. The diagnosis was still uncertain in spite of two more years of specialist examinations. There was some slight variation of symptoms; some days were better than others.

A few years ago, we were driving from Barcelona to Biarritz via the southern border of France. As we turned the corner of France, heading in the direction of the Spanish border, we were close to Marseille. I could see a big church on top of a hill in the middle of the large city, which was built around the harbor at the corner of the bay. There were various medium-sized buildings lining the harbor, mostly hotels, apartment houses, and small office buildings. Bobbing in the harbor were numerous ships of all sizes, from rowboats to large motor launches to big old-fashioned sailing vessels. We could see outdoor cafes in Marseille sitting quietly on the edge of the water; it was about 11:00am, a little before lunchtime, so the cafes were not crowded yet; a few patrons were sitting at tables reading newspapers and enjoying small cups of coffee and other refreshments.

Flags were flying and snapping in the brisk breeze; the scene was very sunny. It was many miles further on to Biarritz, and seeing all the cafes waiting for us stimulated our appetites, so we decided to drive into Marseilles to have lunch. Our road had merged with the city streets and we were already into the main part of the city, which had a quaint, colorful, and inviting air. The city was clean, busy, picturesque, and charming. We drove along, inspecting the cafes, and finally stopped at a colorful two-storied building with an open-air terrace on the second floor. We parked the car and walked along the harbor for a few blocks. We went into an inviting cafe and were shown to a table on the edge of the terrace, with a magnificent view of the bay, the harbor, the big hill with its church on top, and many local streets. The cafe and the streets were getting steadily more crowded -- the lunch hub-bub had started.

We ordered onion soup and filets of sole, both excellent, and we very much enjoyed our stop here. For a few minutes after lunch we enjoyed a short stroll in the harbor district, although my difficulty moving was a nuisance. Marseille does not have much of a reputation as a tourist spot, but it was much more benign, pleasant, interesting, and comfortable than I had expected and might in the future be attractive and inviting for a visit of a few days.

After lunch we drove on to the city of Biarritz and immediately saw our goal, the Hotel du Palais, standing on a small cliff by the Ocean. A large, magnificent, and ornate building, it had been a gift to the Empress Eugénie from her husband, Napoleon III of France, and was later reconfigured as a grand hotel. We had large rooms facing directly on the ocean. The atmosphere was so lovely we decided to have our dinner at the hotel. Sitting among the potted palms in the beautiful dining room, overlooking the Atlantic Ocean, while enjoying the hotel's string quartet and enjoying the excellent dinner, was like a trip into the past. We could almost sense Louis Napoleon and his Eugénie at the next table.

The next day we went sight-seeing and wandered down south, soon crossing the border into Spain, and then reaching Bilbao, with its new and fantastic Guggenheim Museum. This is one of several Guggenheim Museums built in various locations as branches of the Guggenheim Museum of New York. I was surprised by how big the building is, but built in the same style as the others -- like a

234

gigantic pile of empty tin cans. The art works inside are the same standard "modern" art pieces seen at museums all over the world -- more or less. Feeling about to be overcome by ennui at looking at these same old tired items, we left the museum and then saw about a hundred yards to the south a large dog, perhaps a hundred feet high, made of bunches of flowers. This dog was looking out to sea, apparently not interested in the (so-called) art works inside the museum. The dog was the only non-dreary item I saw at the museum and it was attracting lots of smiling attention.

But my main interest in traveling to this locale was to visit the grotto reputed to be the site of the appearance of the Virgin Mary to Bernadette Soubirous (1844-1879), the local peasant girl who became Saint Bernadette of Lourdes. Bernadette herself described this apparition as a "beautiful lady," never claiming that it was the Virgin Mary or any other being. The "lady" appeared to Bernadette fourteen times and was widely believed to be the Virgin Mary. Bernadette's incredulous religious advisors requested that she should ask the Lady her name. The Lady replied to Bernadette's question, "I am the Immaculate Conception," words and concept unknown to the simple Bernadette.

This was not enough to persuade the local priests that something really special and unusual was in their midst, and so they asked Bernadette to request the Lady to give them a sign that she was really a divine messenger. The Lady told Bernadette to dig a hole in the dry floor of the entrance of the grotto and a perpetual spring would appear. All were skeptical of course. Bernadette dug with her hands for some time where she had been instructed to dig. Nothing happened. As she was about to give up, a trickle of water appeared and then slowly increased in volume to a freely flowing spring. As there had never been any water there before, all were mystified and then were impressed that they were witnessing a supernatural event: the Virgin's response to the request for a sign of her presence. This spring still flows at the entrance to the grotto more than a hundred years after its first appearance and is the source of the holy water dispensed at the grotto.

When I was ten years old, I saw the movie "Song of Bernadette," a presentation of these events and the story of Bernadette's life. I would suppose that many people know of the events portrayed and that the grotto had become a site of pilgrimage for those devout (or otherwise) people hoping for a miraculous cure from various serious illnesses.

Over the years, among the millions of visitors and pilgrims, there had been a number of miraculous cures, attributed to the intercession of the Virgin Mary. These cures had been carefully collected by the Church and scrupulously investigated -- including investigations by the "Devil's Advocate." The records are kept at the shrine. The Church is very careful not to accept hearsay evidence, or "cures" which could just be coincidences. The Church does not want to become a gossip factory or a source for unsubstantiated or superstitious tales, especially for situations as serious and somber as these.

I was reminded that forty or fifty years ago, when I was a medical student in New York, it was reported that there were twelve separate, individual patients in the New York vicinity who had been suffering from terminal melanomas. They were all close to death. Suddenly, and without explanation or expectation, these patients individually had a reversal in the course of their illnesses and fully recovered from their terminal cancers. These cases were startling and were thoroughly investigated medically. There was no common treatment or other known factors to account for the cures, and none could be found. These patients were not uniformly religious or devout or members of the same denomination or otherwise alike. No explanation could be discovered, and the patients themselves offered a wide variety of conjectures (or no explanation) as to what had caused their cures. They were not widely reported, but all these were cases of seemingly "miraculous" cures.

I had accepted for many years that there might be incursions into our everyday lives of highly unusual, unlikely, or seemingly miraculous or impossible events which could remain unexplained, including events such as these mysterious cures. According to my reading, these "miraculous" events were not predictable and occurred in people of all characters and conditions, not apparently being "rewards" for being devoutly religious, or religious at all. In addition, there are the occasional almost unbelievable events which are so far out of the ordinary that we can hardly contemplate them, such as dying and then being restored to life.

But this left my own situation: an unexplained, slowly progressive, serious and incapacitating disorder, for which no cause (after five years of careful investigation by eminent medical specialists), or effective treatment had been discovered. I felt that any possible recovery or halt to the progression of my condition needed a miraculous cure, or else likely no cure of any kind would occur. What should I do? I somehow had preserved the hope that I would continue to be able to play, at least somewhat, until the end of my life. If not, then I could accept and adjust to the fact that I would be crippled for the duration, but that would definitely be a less desirable solution. The only possible avenue for improvement I saw was a visit to Lourdes as a medical pilgrim, hoping for a cure there.

We flew from New York to Berlin and then by easy stages by plane and auto to Husum - Hamburg - Toulouse - and on to Lourdes. I felt increasingly cheerful and thought this was now the final attempt to ameliorate or eliminate my condition. I am not sure why I felt that this was to be my ultimate chance to improve/cure my condition, but I definitely had the expectancy that a significant improvement was on the horizon.

We made reservations at the Grand Hotel Moderne in Lourdes and were assigned corner rooms overlooking the nightly candlelight procession starting at the grotto by those hoping for a cure, or an improvement. I hoped for a cure, or a miraculous intervention, but had a feeling that these were not very likely.

However, I then recalled that about thirty-five years ago I had been relieved of a very serious nicotine addiction. This required two hospitalizations in a hospital in the Napa Valley; also the willingness to endure months of discomfort. My first attempt was a failure, but the second attempt (January 23, 1985) resulted in my current condition: many years of relief from that addiction.

A similar result happened when I tried to withdraw from drinking. I had been consuming a quart of gin each evening, which had caused severe and protracted painful hangovers. Many, many attempts to moderate these two addictions had been total failures.

My current sobriety began forty-one years ago (March 5, 1977) and still continues. I know that both these addictions are still alive and are very dangerous, ready to resume their devastation if I ever took even one drink or smoked even one cigarette. So far I have been able to avoid both these situations, akin to keeping the door closed on a cage with cobras inside. A moment's forgetting or lack of attention could be fatal for me.

In my opinion, the relief from these two addictions are genuinely miraculous, and I am very grateful.

Wanting to reach Lourdes, we rented a car for the final two-hour leg of the trip to Lourdes, which is in the foothills of the Pyrenees. The scenery was bucolic, and mountains were in the far distance. The sky was clear.

About thirty minutes after we left from Hamburg bound for Toulouse, I noticed through the windshield an odd object. It was about two or three hundred feet long. It was perhaps thirty or forty feet thick and was rounded at both ends, somewhat in the same shape as a cigar. Flying along at a distance from my car of about five hundred feet and about five hundred feet above the car, its flight paralleled the car and stayed at the same speed. There did not appear to be any windows or wings. Occasionally it would suddenly ascend two or three thousand feet and would travel at this new altitude for a while until it would again suddenly descend. The craft seemed to be "aware" of my car, but did not seem to try to signal or guide the car. The sky was clear and there were no clouds. There were about six glowing colorful lights arranged in two parallel rows. The lights were on for about three seconds and then off for the same amount of time, in a random distribution. There was no sound coming from the craft. There was no indication of a human (or other) intelligence guiding or associated with the craft, and I did not have the impression that there was any attempt to communicate. But I definitely had the impression that the craft had some kind of connection with my car. I had no idea what I was watching.

I had never seen anything like this and when I pointed it out to my travel companion, he was astonished. Neither of us was frightened. There had been from time to time reports of Unknown Flying Objects (UFOs), perhaps flying craft from outside our earth or solar system. I had no explanation as to the nature of what we had seen. After travelling in tandem with us for about ten minutes, the craft began to accelerate and was shortly out of sight, travelling past the horizon in a straight line, and we did not see it again.

As we approached Lourdes, there were some usual type roadside establishments. I noticed a large sign about one hundred yards off the road and up a slight hill, pointing to a medium-sized building fetchingly named "MILORD DISCO." As we did not visit this establishment, I cannot give any report on its charms, but am happy to say it was not characteristic of the commercial establishments along the way. There was no element of tawdry establishments or of emporiums of high-priced junk, nor anything suggestive of Coney Island or loud blaring music.

By 8pm we found our hotel, the Grande Hotel Moderne, perhaps the best hotel in town, in the center of Lourdes and were shown to our spacious, very clean, air-conditioned suite. We noticed that there were special pink wheel-chair lanes painted on the streets, and we saw thousands of wheel chairs and gurneys being pushed around the streets.

There was another type of vehicle, previously unknown to me. These were called "patient wagons," with a platform on wheels carrying a rectangular platform with a little fence around the perimeter. A wheel chair was fastened to top of the rear section of this platform and carried a single patient. There was a long wooden tongue sticking out in front, pulled by a single person, while a second person pushed from the back.

We decided to go out for a short stroll. and found the streets filled with shops selling religious items: carved and painted wooden figures of Jesus, the Virgin Mary, creche scenes with lambs and camels and mangers, crucifixes, rosaries; all were in a wide variety of sizes and styles and all were nicely carved. There were many bottles, both painted and plain, to hold the holy water bubbling up from the spring in the holy grotto; these ranged in size from ten cc to several gallons. All the religious goods stores seemed to be doing a brisk business, but there were no hawkers roaming the streets or the stores. I purchased several wooden icons and little wooden animals as gifts for myself and for my friends at home. We saw a notice that the nightly candlelight procession was scheduled for 8:30pm, starting at the holy grotto.

The dining room at the hotel opened at 6pm, and we decided to have an early dinner. The dining room, somewhat cavernous and high-ceilinged, with dark brown carved and coffered ceiling, was mostly occupied by tables seating eight or ten guests. The room and the tables were almost completely filled by convivial groups appearing to be previously acquainted members of tour groups. We were asked what diocese we were representing, and on being at a loss for an answer (which was truthfully, "None."), were directed to a table seating two. Apparently most guests came as members of larger church or other groups, but there was accommodation for smaller groups or even one or two persons. The service was prompt and polite. Wine was available, and we noticed a number of guests enjoying wines probably from local vineyards, for which France is famous. Dinner was served automatically, without ordering, first course was a vegetable soup; the main course consisted of meatballs in tomato sauce, accompanied by broccoli and roasted potatoes, all of which were nicely prepared. Ice cream concluded the meal, which was good enough, considering the large number of simultaneous guests and that the price of the meal was included in the room charge.

As the meal progressed, we could see occasional flurries of activity on the streets and sidewalks -- groups of wheel-chairs or gurneys, all moving in the same direction. We assumed they were all moving towards the holy grotto for the start of the candlelight procession. After a slight discussion, we decided to try to join the procession ourselves. There had been no mention of registering or enrolling to take part. It was apparently open to any who wished to participate.

Steve brought my wheelchair from upstairs, and we started out in the general direction everyone else was moving. We were able to obtain candles, each one surrounded by a paper collar to protect its flame against the wind. Everyone walking with us was carrying a similar candle, and soon the entire field was covered by a snake line composed of a huge number of people with their candles.

In about two hundred yards, as we came close to the holy grotto, the start of the procession, we could see that we were part of a group of about fifty wheelchairs and perhaps fifty gurneys with reclining patients. There were many pushers and helpers for our little group, and a cardinal was walking close by. There were many women dressed somewhat as nurses, who were generally helping the proceedings, and there was a group of about two or three thousand

240

walkers joining with us. There were many other similar groups of wheelchairs and walkers. I estimated that the total number of people in the procession was about fifty thousand. The entire field was covered by this huge crowd walking slowly in a snake line while carrying their votive candles.

Soon prayers and religious music from loudspeakers began, and continued for the next two hours. Somehow there was a subdued and lovely atmosphere. The procession began about 8:40 and was directed by officials both at the head of the procession as well as along the way. We could see other groups of wheelchairs, gurneys, patient wagons, and regular walkers-pilgrims. There was no noise or raucous behavior. Everyone involved was in a serious or devout, but not exactly somber or gloomy mood. This was a religious procession, not a demonstration or a protest. As the procession slowly moved along, officials motioned some participants to go left or go right. Because of this attrition, we finally found ourselves at the head of the procession and exactly in the center of the first row. The procession was halted at this point.

The holy grotto was just under the cathedral, where a stage or platform had been built and which was the location for the rest of the ceremony, which consisted of songs, prayers, and some other invocations, and which lasted just under an hour. Seats were brought for the numerous handicapped people, like me, and we were seated for the rest of the service. Soon it began to rain softly, then harder, and finally there was a downpour which lasted the rest of the service, dousing the remaining candles. Frequent close-by lightning strikes added to the consternation of the crowd. The women helpers brought plastic covers to protect us. The crowd was so dense and the topography of the location was so hilly, uneven, and unfamiliar that the crowd stayed in place -- only a very few of the thousands of participants could be seen leaving, even in the midst of the rain and lightning storm.

I began to be slightly frightened, as I had several previous close calls with lightning, including the death of a great grandfather who was hit and killed by lightning and several strikes on my country home in Danbury, Connecticut, including one on my brass bed in the bedroom. The lightning, after hitting the corner of the house, passed down into the ground and then radiated out, digging two channels in

241

the ground, each about three feet wide and three feet deep and two hundred feet long I had witnessed the tremendous power of the lightning strikes.

In other words, the procession here in Lourdes, which had started so serenely, concluded with frightening lightning and thunder. Sturm und Drang. It was almost miraculous that the lightning strikes didn't hit someone. But it was a memorable occasion.

The next day we drove around the city and its environs, visited the cathedral, which was built on top of the mountain above the holy grotto. We did some shopping for souvenirs and gifts. We had lunch at Lourdes branch of McDonalds, which was about the same as any other McDonalds. Our hamburgers were delicious.

The visit to Lourdes was one of the oddest travel experiences I ever had. It was more pleasant and interesting than I had anticipated, and I would recommend a visit there as a matter of general interest, but I doubt that it is a place I will ever visit again. I am not aware that a healing miracle occurred for me, but perhaps it will manifest later. My last memory on driving away from Lourdes was seeing the hundreds of wheelchairs again rolling around the streets in their special pink lanes.

It was about a thirty minute drive to the Lourdes airport, a new and modern building with very little activity at that day and hour, although the giant crowds attending the religious ceremonies must put the place to good use at other times.

It was a one hour flight to Paris, which is certainly a beautiful, elegant city, and it seemed like going to another world.

Chapter 18

Paris

Lourdes is one of the most concentrated, intense spiritual locations on earth. Paris's atmosphere is almost totally different, although the sense of history, grandeur, and importance is almost palpable. And I always forget just how beautiful the city is, truly breathtaking.

The flight from Lourdes to Paris was about one hour. When the plane was descending into the Charles de Gaulle Airport at Paris, we had a clear view of the Eiffel Tower, a symbol of Paris. I felt a thrill of excitement when I saw this famous structure. The airport seems to always run smoothly even though it is one of the world's busiest, and so within an hour we had retrieved our baggage and were installed in a large SUV type car which we had pre-ordered to transport us and our eight big suitcases.

I recalled my first visit to the Ritz and to Paris, with my mother, about thirty years previously. Then, the atmosphere was quite tense when we arrived. Large army tanks were stationed on many of the streets, some streets were closed, and two big army tanks were parked in the middle of the Place Vendôme, just in front of the Ritz. This was my first trip to Paris and my first trip to Europe, so I did not realize how unusual the situation was. The problem, a very serious one, was that France was expecting an invasion by Algerian armed forces, concerning an escalated quarrel between France and Algeria over the matter of Algeria's independence from France. The conflict was peacefully resolved, the tanks were removed, and no armed invasion took place. I had been barely aware that this situation, potentially catastrophic, was occurring around me. Later I understood. The Ritz had remained an island of tranquility and propriety through the crisis. As if this were not enough excitement, one night I went out, met a young man in a bar, went home with him, and had my pocket cleverly picked, which I only discovered to my chagrin the next morning. I told my mother a sad story, and she kindly replenished my money supply, no questions asked. Oh, well. But back to the present:

The drive from the airport into Paris took about one hour, and when we arrived at the Ritz Hotel, several bellboys took our bags and directed us to the registration desk. It felt like coming home to enter the Ritz again, very safe and very comfortable (no revolution or invasions here!!), with prices to match, of course. The reception desk had been moved slightly and reoriented, and the reception room, at the very front of the hotel had been reconstructed, and several large windows had been installed, giving a more open and well-lit air. Previously there had been no windows in the reception room, giving a slightly compressed effect.

The Ritz Hotel, named after its founder, Cesar Ritz, opened in Paris on the Place Vendôme in 1898, as a very deluxe establishment. Over the years it has been open, it has served both as a hotel and also as a refuge and sanctuary for very special groups, including many of the Russian aristocrats, both before and after the Russian revolution, other royal persons, movie stars, and a wide group of celebrated and/or famous persons.

Princess Diana left the Ritz in her car for her final, fatal excursion. Coco Chanel had lived in the Ritz, in a large deluxe suite overlooking the Place Vendôme, for the duration of the entire Second World War -- I have been told that she was a guest (presumably the mistress) of the German commandant of Paris. She did not need to pay any bills at the hotel. As a Jewish woman, to have lived through the War in this condition in this hotel is almost unbelievable -- she must have been very charmingly attractive. The only situation somewhat similar, was the survival through the second

World War of Gertrude Stein and her lover, Alice B. Toklas, (both were Jewish Lesbians), indolently residing in the French countryside.

For several years (later on) I often saw Chanel having her lunch, sometimes dining alone, other times usually with a male companion, in one of the Ritz restaurants. She appeared very serious, almost somber, but elegant and with an atmosphere of melancholy. Her main shop in Paris, where she worked every day, is just across the Rue Cambon, on the side of the Ritz facing away from the Vendôme. At that time, I stayed in the Ritz frequently and often passed by Madame Chanel in the lobbies -- we eventually began to speak and nod in greeting. Needless to say, she was always dressed most beautifully, in an understated style, but she always seemed almost severe in her expression, at the same time very graceful. Many other people of note also regularly stayed in the Ritz, Hemingway for example, as well as Marlene Dietrich, Greta Garbo, the Aga Khan, and various other royal personages.

Right across the Vendôme is the apartment where Chopin died -- it is marked by a small plaque (This is the place described in my section "Havana After Midnight" in Chapter 11, Book III of this Memoir, in which the Princess Marceline Czartoryska holds Chopin as he dies.).

The Ritz was part of the perimeter of the Place Vendôme. The relatively low buildings of the Place (generally about six or seven stories) were similar or almost identical and made a very harmonious picture. The hotel was just part of this facade, not a separate building, and was distinguished by three small canopies covering archways pierced in the facade. Just inside the arches was a small driveway or port cochere where visitors to the hotel could be received under cover. These canopies had very discreet markings, "Ritz." Otherwise there was no marking identifying the hotel. The windows of the upper stories of the hotel appeared to be part of the general pattern and blended in perfectly with the rest of the windows in the entire facade encircling the Place. It was a beautiful and dignified structure; and a very appropriate introduction to what lay inside.

The hotel was built on a rectangular plan, rather like the shape of a domino, the short sides facing the Place Vendôme (the front of the hotel) and the Rue Cambon (the back of the hotel), and the long sides of the domino running from the front of the hotel to its rear. This made an enclosed long rectangular space, which was planted with a beautiful garden. Immediately adjoining this arrangement was a second equally sized and shaped domino, also enclosing a rectangular garden. These two beautifully planted, colorful connecting gardens were available for the use of the guests of the Ritz, sometimes for strolling, other times for sitting, sometimes for dining. Just inside the hotel building, running parallel to the long wall, and the same length as this wall, was an extensive display, in glass cases running along both sides of the domino, of various luxury items displayed for sale in their respective hotel shops, such as scarves, neckties, clothing, jewelry, furniture, books, maps, perfumes and cosmetics. There was usually a policeman patrolling this valuable display, also a clerk who could unlock the various cases and tell the various prices. To stroll along this passage, looking at the various displays, required about thirty minutes.

Underneath these dominoes a spa had been constructed a few years ago. There was a sizeable swimming pool, and its ceiling was beautifully painted with clouds and sky.

The various dining rooms of the Ritz offered luxurious and attractive surroundings, excellent service, and delicious food. Both the dining room experience and the room service were perfect. Like most very fine restaurants, both dining room and room service produced a feeling of safety and extreme well-being. The Hemingway Bar, on the Cambon side of the hotel, is the most famous of the bars, having been a favorite watering hole of the famous author. I gave a few small cocktail parties and small dinner parties over the years in some of these rooms, or in my suite, always perfectly produced; and what delights they were.

The entire hotel had just finished a refurbishment project and gave the appearance of being both old and new at the same time. The furniture no longer had any nicks or scrapes, but appeared to be old, antique furniture in perfect condition, as if new. The walls had been treated to new silk wall coverings; the gilded electrical switches were all perfect, as if newly made; the fine carpets and heavy draperies were all immaculate. The bathrooms had newly installed, modern shower stalls as well as very large bathtubs. The sinks and the tubs had old-fashioned gilded water spouts in the shape of swans with wings half-spread.

The table call-device still had buttons to call the waiter, the room servant, and the bellboy, but these were now electronic rather than mechanical. The halls and lobbies were pristine and very attractive, as were the dining rooms and the bar. One of the few differences from the former hotel was the absence of the delicate small benches which had been in all the elevators. All in all, the hotel had done a magnificent job of refreshing and renewing their premises, and without disturbing its history or memories.

Another very nice hotel in Paris was the Crillon, which had been shuttered at the same time as the Ritz, and for the same purpose. We wanted to see how that hotel had managed to improve or maintain itself, and so we took a taxi to the Place Concorde, another of the main centers of Paris, about a half-mile from the Place Vendôme. We were disappointed to see that their "upgrade" had been done in modern style, as if we were in the bus station, and we were glad to be staying in our hotel, which seemed to us much more attractive.

Our suite, #517, was on the top floor and had a view of some of the taller buildings in Paris, as well as of the gardens down below. I was feeling tired from the travels, and so after a short rest, we had dinner in our rooms. On retiring for the night, I remembered that the Ritz always had the most comfortable beds I had ever experienced. Heavenly.

The next day we visited the Guimet Museum, an outstanding museum of Asian art. They have a very fine collection of Indian stone carvings, some very large and impressive, as well as many beautiful Tibetan and Indian bronzes, both gilded and plain. This is one of my favorite museums anywhere; I always like to visit this museum when I am in Paris. We had a very good lunch on a lower floor and then returned to our hotel for a nap.

We had heard from my cousin Kris Kvam and his wife Mehera that they would be in Paris when we were there and so had made an appointment to have lunch together at the Jules Verne Restaurant on the middle level of the Eiffel Tower.

Kris had graduated from West Point a few years earlier, and he had then been stationed as a military attaché to the embassy in

Maputo, Mozambique. He married his brilliant and charming fiancé, Mehera, in Washington D.C. and after his tour of duty in Maputo finished, he was reassigned to the US for a short rest, and then he and Mehera were posted to the embassy in Conakry, Guinea. They were in Paris for a few days as part of their vacation and their transit from the US to Guinea. Kris was my cousin, and I was always glad to see him. Charming, brilliant, and handsome, his career was advancing, and he was one of the few people I knew who seemed destined to have a fine and interesting life. Mehera was a good partner for him and she was herself involved in an advancing and growing technical governmental career. They would be living somewhat apart in Africa due to their respective jobs, but would be together frequently at various African locations.

The lunch at the Eiffel Tower was very interesting, the food was delicious, and the view was of course spectacular. Kris and Mehera and Steve and I had a very pleasant visit. I was a little sad to say goodbye, because at my age of eighty-four the prospect of future visits is not assured. "Farewell," we said, and gave each other hugs, and then went our separate ways back into Paris and on course for our journey to the future.

Two days later we were approaching the end of our trip, and we decided to visit the Fragonard Museum of fragrances. The Museum is somewhat hidden away, but a group of about forty people was assembled for a tour of the premises, comprising three large show rooms.

Perfumes and colognes are made in this venue, and several huge alembics and other distillation equipment occupied a substantial part of the main room, and other complicated devices were placed about, appearing to be parts of a very complex manufacturing setup. These rooms were also used as sales rooms.

The host of the visit gave us a very detailed account and explanation of the manufacture of various types of fragrances and their strengths/concentrations and uses. About thirty different fragrances, in their various forms, were offered for sale in various sizes. Most of the visitors purchased a few different sizes and types of fragrance. Some of the shadow people were moved by this display, remembering the fragrances from long ago in Danbury, Connecticut.

Years ago I had discovered that a few drops of fragrance placed on my pillow would sometimes cause interesting variations in my dreams, and I looked forward to dreamy experimentations with my beautiful new fragrances. I didn't want to break the seals and open the bottles before I got back home, so later on I carefully packed them in my suitcases -- they all arrived safely in New York, and I have used them to give me some very pleasant, fragrant dreams.

I look forward to visiting Paris again in the not too distant future.

Some of the shadow people also look forward to my next visit, as do the various revenants and partial spirits waiting there.

John Loomis, M.D.

Chapter 19

Predation

When I answered the intercom telephone in my apartment, the doorman at the front door downstairs informed me, "You have a visitor. Mildred Bent is here to see you."

"Please send her up," I replied. I had been expecting her, and she was here exactly on time. One of my friends, hearing me complain about my physical problems, mainly increasing problems in playing the piano, had told me about an advisor who had helped him last year. He said she was very experienced in physical problems of this kind, and he knew of friends who had been helped by her. He told me that she preferred not to see patients in her office, but instead liked to see them at their homes, and suggested that I could call Mrs. Bent at her office.

The next day I called her and we had a brief and pleasant conversation, during which I told her a short summary of my problem, and we made an appointment to meet the next week at my apartment. Now the appointment had arrived, and I was hopeful and enthusiastic about the meeting.

Mildred Bent was very nicely and neatly dressed, appeared about fifty years old, had a firm handshake and looked me directly in the eye as we introduced ourselves. She looked athletic and moved without difficulty. She seated herself on the sofa, and I couldn't help noticing that her short skirt rode rather high on her thighs when she sat down. It turned out that this was the case at all of our meetings. I felt somewhat embarrassed by this, but of course decided to say nothing. She asked me many questions about the onset and course of my condition and was obviously very intelligent and experienced in this matter.

She asked me to demonstrate precisely my piano playing difficulty, which was of course easy to show her -- some hesitation in playing, along with slight difficulty bending one of my fingers. After just a few minutes, I always found playing quite tiring. I had been extensively examined by a wide variety of experts, and they all said that either they could not find anything wrong with me, or that my difficulty was caused by disuse.

It is difficult to live in New York and engage in ordinary daily activity without considerable usage of the hands and arms, and I practiced the piano faithfully at least two hours daily, so I was not persuaded by the disuse hypothesis, but I had no other or better explanation. There had been no trauma or illness to start off this condition, which had been slowly progressing over the last five years, but some days were better than others. Nothing seemed to help this condition; neither did any activity seem to make me worse, but lack of sleep and general fatigue added to this problem.

Mildred did some tests of muscle strength and gave me some mild strengthening exercises in the hope that perhaps they might be of help. The session had lasted about ninety minutes, and before we parted we made arrangements to meet again in about a month. I felt the meeting had been cordial and had been a success. I was hopeful for some improvement or good result from the exercises, and looked forward to our next meeting.

A month later the next meeting followed the same format, began with a cordial handshake, a kiss on my mouth, and was marked by pleasant and interesting conversation, and again lasted about ninety minutes. Mildred carefully checked my exercise form, asked many questions, and was encouraging as to the possibility of future improvement. We shook hands again at the end of the meeting. After several monthly meetings, we began to exchange friendly but casual hugs, and less casual kisses on the mouth at the start and finish of the meetings. These kisses were instituted and directed by Mildred.

I hoped that the meetings would not start to be preludes to anticipated (by Mildred) physical, romantic, or other contacts of an intimate nature with Mildred Bent. I recalled that sometimes women seemed to expect that their relationships with me would soon morph into a sexual affair, and they might even be angry if I did not comply with their wishes/demands. Although Mildred knew that I was a gay man (because of reading the first two volumes of this memoir), I was not sure that this knowledge would serve as adequate blockade against any possible sexual aggression on her part. Many women can't really believe that any man would decline their favors -- he just needs to be shown the way.

I am anxious about physical contacts with people I don't know well, but these contacts with Mildred Bent seemed innocent and not inappropriate. After all, I knew that I would not be trying to expand or sexualize the contact, and the meetings got their start for truly therapeutic purposes. In spite of this, I was acutely aware of, uncomfortable and sensitive to the nuances of our greeting and parting rituals and kisses.

The next meeting was about a month later and followed the same format. The meetings did not have any fixed duration, but were getting longer and longer. I had a hard time bringing the meetings to an end. It seemed to me, after some reflection, that I subliminally felt that it was hostile, or at least unfriendly, for me to bring a meeting to a conclusion. This attitude was of course pathological on my part, but was an invitation to Mildred to attempt to control our meetings. It turned out that she was practiced in controlling others.

I think our original plan was that the meetings would last about an hour, but they were now extending to three or four hours. Only once did Mildred conclude the meeting; all other times they went on until I concluded the session. Although the meetings seemed cordial, and the prescribed exercises were helping a little with the piano problems, I began to find the sessions taxing and somewhat tense. Mildred would come in, we would hug and kiss, she would seat herself on the sofa and begin to talk. There was usually some passing comment about my physical problem, but the meetings soon became primarily social. Sometimes Mildred would ask me how I was, other times she would not ask, or there might be no mention at all of our therapeutic purpose. In fairness, I talked about 10% of the time, and Mildred held forth about 90% of the time.

Soon I asked Steve if he would come into my apartment about 90 minutes after the beginning of a session, so as to help bring the session to a close. I would tell Mildred, or she would ask me, if I had an appointment for dinner this evening. She seemed to indicate that in her mind this was a legitimate reason for finishing the session.

Our usual goodbye ritual would feature a firm and perhaps inappropriately lengthy kiss on my mouth. I tried to turn my head away, but my efforts were usually circumvented by Mildred's increasingly agile and determined moves. I was growing increasingly uncomfortable and embarrassed by this kissing arrangement, but I didn't know how to control it or better still how to avoid it altogether. As a gay man, I was absolutely certain that the kissing was neither welcome to me nor invited by me.

The news lately had featured reported predations by many famous Hollywood actors and other prominent public and entertainment figures against underage girls or women who were of legal age but had been coerced into being unwilling sexual or physical partners for the predatory men. The episodes of reported sexual predation were always portrayed as power moves performed by men against women. The men involved were named, openly criticized, and the men were usually fired, resigned, or otherwise lost their jobs. I never saw any reports of sexual predation by women against men. Perhaps men were even more embarrassed than women by being victims of sexual bullying, and so they were too ashamed to complain.

There was a sexual stereotype that bothered me: No reasonable virile or normally sexual he-man would ever decline, much less run away from, an offer of sexual contact from any woman, no matter what the characteristics of the woman, or the type of sexual contact or the situation at the time. If he did, he must be an utter sissy, fop, or fag -- labels which I did not wish to struggle against, particularly if the woman in question was someone who had just figuratively castrated me and who enjoyed openly showing her contempt and scorn, a rather common reaction.

As time went on, Mildred's bullying persisted, perhaps becoming slightly more pronounced. Never did I detect any hesitation on Mildred's part about determinedly pursuing her goals with me, although exactly what the goals were was never explicitly stated. Some kind of sexual contact I assumed, at least the vigorous kissing.

After about eighteen months of this relationship, Mildred had a change in her schedule. We could no longer meet in the late afternoon; our appointments would be changed to 1:30pm. I was pleased about this change, as the meetings would be more of a daytime activity, rather than an evening activity, with the corresponding closer proximity to a range of night time activities.

One of my neighbors, Alice Robinson, who was likewise an expert in physical training, told me she had just read a wonderful book called "Neighbors Together." Alice was recently widowed after a fifteen-year marriage, was well-to-do, and seemed in excellent physical condition. She was attractive, intelligent, well educated, very energetic, well-to-do, and had run her own therapeutic meetings. But she told me that she had been lonely since her late husband died, and she was hoping to meet a man. Her dog had recently been put to sleep, and when I asked her if she intended to get another dog, she brightly replied, "First a man, and then a dog." She had plainly and openly declared herself to be on the hunt. No surprise.

She said that the men she met initially seemed attractive, but then something always went wrong and showed them to be unsuitable for her. I had known Alice for some years and realized that most men would find her impossibly bossy, dictatorial, intrusive, and not adequately forthright.

She invited us to spend a weekend at her country house, but we declined politely. Later she told us that she recorded and transcribed the conversations of her house guests (without their knowledge) to illustrate in her forthcoming book cross currents in the developing relationships of previously unacquainted guests. In other words, we were invited to her house to be guinea pigs or specimens in her forthcoming psychology book.

Another time she highly recommended a new telephone company and vigorously tried to push us into signing up with them, which we didn't accept. Two months later she inadvertently told us that the new company would give her a month's free service for every new client she could obtain for them. In other words, she wanted to surreptitiously make money on us -- to hell with our phone service I assumed.

This was the kind of sly and dishonest manipulation which made me recoil, as I had much experience of this earlier in life, and right up to the present, as described here. If we had fallen for her lines, Alice would probably have thought herself admirably clever. There were other maneuvers of this kind. Long ago we had developed a distrust of Alice, although in other ways she was a good neighbor.

One day we arrived home to find a copy of "Neighbors Together" lying against the front door. Alice had previously highly praised this book to us. It was a quick read, describing two adult single people of late middle age, both recently widowed after lengthy happy marriages, both living alone in the same neighborhood. Their houses were close together. They were both lonely and so they decided to sleep together every night, sex was optional, and marriage was not in the plan: it was purely a companionship arrangement for two lonely people. Hint, hint (except I was not lonely). It worked out quite well for the characters in the book, sex was immediately featured in their relationship, but they eventually drifted apart due to other realistic circumstances. I was not inspired to follow the example of the resourceful characters in the book, and was slightly offended by the blunt nature of this solicitation.

Alice seemed to have a darker side to her psyche. Once I heard her mutter, "The turds of desire have an alluring fragrance." Not believing what I had just heard, I said, "Pardon me?" Alice began to hum and whistle, and then said, "Never mind. I was just working on a song I have been composing." No more was said, but from then on I knew that Alice had a very strange part of her psyche.

For the last thirty years of my life, I have frequently been mistaken for a fish waiting to be caught. Usually I can see the hook coming from far off -- the women get a distinctive expression on their faces -- I call it the "predation readiness look." I am not flattered by this attempted trickery and/or aggression. Now, several years later, I am still angry when I think about these dishonest coercive attempts, and I recall this lingering anger as a feature of the stories of the women who were victims of predation.

One afternoon, just after we had moved the meeting time to early afternoon, I arrived home at 5:30pm (the previous meeting time) to find that I had missed (forgotten) the 1:30pm appointment with Mildred. I was embarrassed by my carelessness and called her right away to apologize and to suggest that we set another appointment in the near future.

"Oh, no," she said, I will call you soon and we can set a time for our next appointment." As of now, three months later, I have not heard from her and have not tried to contact her. I hope this is the end of our relationship. She helped me somewhat with the piano problem, and caused me to have more hope about it than previously, and for this I am grateful. I am sorry that the relationship took a turn into the shadows. Steve, who has a good nose for pretense and fakery, said that the current long silence from Mildred was designed to arouse my interest and curiosity. I rather sourly commented that this was a piece of bad judgment, as I had no inclination ever to revitalize the contact.

And so life events progressed, like running down a football field dodging the tacklers.

The purpose of leaving this book, "Neighbors Together" for me (and Steve) to read was painfully obvious. Although neither Steve nor I were interested, I felt the gesture was quite sad. No more was said about it. I thought this lack of response might be the end of Alice's attempts to snare me as her next "companion." Wrong, more similar maneuvers were produced. I thought "slave" might be a more appropriate label for what was desired. Alice and Mildred were acquainted. I do not know if they were co-conspirators. I would not be pleased to be captured by either of these ladies. I felt lucky to have escaped another trap.

A slightly different version of this dishonesty involved my dentist, of whom I had been a patient for many years.

One evening I suddenly developed a severe pain in the right side of my upper jaw. The next morning the pain was worse, and I called my regular dentist. He was away on vacation, and his practice was being covered by his son, Junior Dentist. On seeing the son, he took an X-ray and told me I had a serious abscess, and the affected tooth needed to have a root canal. I asked him if he was experienced in such matters, and he answered "Of course," and proceeded to do the root canal, telling me to return in three days so he could check on my progress. Early in the night the pain returned, worse than ever.

In the morning I called Dr. Junior to tell him what had happened. He irritably told me, "I told you not to eat candy with your tooth." I told him that I had not eaten any candy. Actually, he had never said a word about not eating anything, but graciously made an appointment to see me in three days. I wondered how I could stand three more days of this very severe pain. I called some friends experienced in dental problems, and they referred me to their dentist. When I saw Dr. New, he took more X-rays and then told me the reason I was still having pain was that Dr. Junior had done his root canal on the wrong tooth, thereby killing it and necessitating doing the procedure over again on the neighboring tooth. I called Dr. Junior to tell him of the situation. He did not apologize, offer any consolation, and generally presented himself as a know-it-all jerk. I wrote him a starchy letter implying that I was going to sue him, which was an idle threat designed to persuade him to behave himself. I found out that my letter worried him. It seemed that his fantasy about being a therapist-healer was on shaky ground, but he had successfully used it to lure me into his den of dental malpractice. He might try a lure more inviting than his mixture of reeking garlic sauce with sauerkraut, Mildred's secret recipe.

"Boo Hoo," I thought. Both teeth survived for the time being. Caveat emptor, dental version.

Whenever I think about Mildred's sexual bullying, I feel angry and resentful. I had known of this reaction in previous victims of sexual harassment, but had never really understood why they would feel this way. I still do not understand why I am so resentful, but the fading feelings of anger and resentment persist.

Perhaps the problem is the unresolved nature of Mildred's aggressive actions. Somewhat surprised that her kisses had not propelled me into her bed, she tried again, forcefully mashing, to the point of pain, her sticky lips, still coated with her favorite snack, fried pork pieces covered with sauerkraut mixed with garlic sauce. I tried to protect my trembling lips behind a piece of heavy cardboard from a Dixie cup. She shrieked in disappointment not to have damaged me.

She definitely did not observe the obligations of therapist to a patient or client, and she used a version of politeness as a covert means of trying to make me do what she wanted. (Hello = Kisskiss, Goodbye = KissKissKissss). I wonder how many other patients she had stressed or disappointed in this way by attempting to make them gratify her desires, but trust I will never know. Sexual bullying is a humiliating and very bad way to treat anyone, particularly someone who is formally trusting that you will try to be of help and will try not to be of harm (as for instance, in the doctor-patient relationship). I survived.

John Loomis, M.D.

Chapter 20

Literary Lions

In the early 1960s I was contacted by my friend Fred Morgan, who wanted to renew our relationship after a prolonged absence. Fred was a native New Yorker and was the founder in 1948 (with his Princeton classmates Joseph Bennett and William Arrowsmith) of the *Hudson Review*, one of the foremost literary quarterlies. Fred was also the magazine's editor. The magazine was highly respected and influential in the literary world.

During the next two or three years, we met occasionally concerning various matters. We both enjoyed these meetings, and a friendship developed. I stood by as a friendly ear as Fred weathered several very significant developments, including some happy events, as well as some tragic ones.

He was a member of an old and prominent New York family, was a Princeton graduate, and was well-connected in both the social and literary worlds. Although sometimes averse to formal social events, he was not shy or socially uneasy.

He was interested in writing and knew many writers because of his work with the *Hudson Review*. Among the earliest contributors to the Review were T. S. Eliot, Ezra Pound, William Carlos Williams, and Joyce Carol Oates, all of whom Fred had known personally as well as professionally. I had been reading the *Hudson Review* for years and was delighted to know Fred and to hear about the magazine and its contributors.

261

After a few years, Fred asked me to join the editorial board, and I was happy to accept this honor. Fred's wife, Paula Deitz Morgan, was now the assistant editor. Paula was herself a brilliant writer and critic and welcomed me as a new member of the board. My role was to read material when requested and make comments or suggestions when appropriate and to attend board meetings.

Occasionally, the Morgans would discuss ideas about the future course of the magazine. Several times they invited me for a visit to their beautiful country home, which was always a great pleasure.

Fred was himself a very gifted writer. He eventually felt it was time to publish his own writings. He overcame his natural reticence, and his first volume of poems, *A Book of Change*, was published in 1972 to very good reviews. It was nominated for a National Book Award.

Sometime later Fred was distressed to hear of the death of his old friend Joseph Bennett, who had been traveling for years in the Far East, and so he very generously decided to establish a prize in his name. Fred and Paula decided that the prize should be awarded every two years to a writer of excellence whose writings had not yet received the reputation they warranted. In addition to the favorable publicity, the writer would also receive a large cash prize. They went ahead with this plan and assembled a group of respected authors to nominate writers and review their works, which could be in any language. Needless to say, this was an extensive and time-consuming job.

I was surprised and pleased to be invited to serve on the board for the new Bennett Award. My role was primarily ceremonial, although I was very interested to follow the judging process as it was going on. I met and talked with almost all the prize winners, usually sitting next to them at the award dinner or ceremony every two years. What follows are my impressions of these very gifted and productive people:

1976. The first Bennett Award was given to the Spanish writer Jorge Guillen. I did not meet him.

1978. The award was given to the Russian writer Andrei Sinyavsky, who wrote under the name Tertz. His works were based on his experiences in Soviet gulags and were quite grim. He was an elderly man with a long beard and a haunted, unsmiling face. Although he was pleasant and polite, he spoke very little, as Russian was his language. He said his English was very poor, so my communication with him was minimal.

1980. V. S. Naipaul. I found him quite articulate, charming, intelligent, and of course a very fine writer. Middle-aged, energetic, and sociable, he wanted to discuss with me the possible ways he could invest his prize money. I told him what I knew, and he was interested in my ideas about the matter. Later on, in 2001, he won the Nobel Prize, and so he had even more funds to invest. I hope he has done well. Some found him too demanding, but I found him refreshingly forthright.

1982. Seamus Heaney, the Irish poet. Intelligent, but rather too forceful and abrupt for my comfort. He seemed athletic and energetic. In 1995 he was awarded the Nobel Prize.

1984. Anthony Powell. Prolific author, including the giant twelve-volume (and fascinating) novel, *A Dance to the Music of Time*. He was a real charmer, as was his wife, the Lady Violet. They had both seen very large sections of life, and they had benign and astute opinions of what they had seen. The award ceremony was held at the American Embassy in London and was attended by many British literary figures, including Lady Antonia Fraser, whose biography of Marie Antoinette had just appeared to fine reviews. She was beautiful, charming, and very intelligent—a real pleasure to meet. She was accompanied by her husband, Harold Pinter, whose reputation was not in any way based on his charm, which was invisible, and he was not a real pleasure to meet. He seemed to me to be a professional grouch. He and Lady Antonia seemed an unlikely couple, but as I once heard a well-known analyst say, "Unconscious calls to unconscious."

1986. Nadine Gordimer. Serious, pleasant, kindly, perceptive, friendly, and charming. She was well-known for her antiapartheid writings, and a few years later, in 1991, she was awarded the Nobel Prize.

1988. Yves Bonnefoy, an outstanding French writer. I was not present for the ceremonies.

1990. William Trevor. Very skillful English short-story writer. I did not have a chance to talk at length with him.

1992. Charles Tomlinson. English poet with stunningly perfect word choice and descriptions. He and his very cordial and attractive wife Brenda invited us to come out from London for a short visit to their country home. Charles gave me a beautiful poem that he had just written concerning my journey and arrival at their station. I was moved and honored. The Tomlinsons seemed to know all the plants in their very lovely garden and were on speaking terms with the birds who came and went. They were obviously deeply in love with each other. This excursion was like a visit to paradise.

1994. Frank Tuohy. English novelist who spent much of his time living out of England or traveling. His writings were concerned with the more somber aspects of modern life.

At this point, the Morgans decided that the Bennett Award had accomplished its goal of promoting very good but underappreciated writers, and so the prize was discontinued. I was sorry to see it close down, thinking it had been very valuable to the honorees, but at the same time realizing what a heavy burden and responsibility the selection process was. It was a fine, beautiful endeavor skillfully carried out, and I was proud to have been associated with the prize.

The list of Bennett Award winners included outstanding and accomplished writers chosen by well-respected authors. This award was primarily honoring the writers, more than any of their individual works.

* * * * *

I decided to assemble another list, this time of works that were influential in my life, generally well written, but primarily of value to me because of their subject matter, perhaps psychological, intellectual, emotional, historical, or spiritual, or otherwise enlightening of obscure or unusual matters, or possibly works in the process of being forgotten (on the path to becoming orphan memories). They are all works that I happened on by chance in the course of reading and listening during the past eighty years. I hope their inclusion on this list rescues any of them from the possible fate of becoming orphan memories, as described previously. This is not a list of authors or creators, but of individual written (or musical) works and includes five very beautiful musical compositions, somewhat obscure masterpieces, one of which was performed for a deceased Russian grand duchess, as described in an earlier chapter. I only claim that these works have been important to me, not that they are supreme artistic creations, although, of course, some of them are that.

1. Carl Gustav Jung: *Memories, Dreams, Reflections.* The story of the growth, development, and maturation of a great psychologist. His *Modern Man in Search of a Soul* is also very wise.

2. Tenzin Gyatso, the Fourteenth Dalai Lama: *Kindness, Clarity, and Insight.* How to conduct one's life in the most constructive and beneficial way possible from the viewpoint of Tibetan Tantric Buddhism. The Dalai Lama is a great and subtle theologian, and this is a profound work.

3. Sangharakshita: *The Eternal Legacy: An Introduction to the Canonical Literature of Buddhism.* Intricate analysis of this subject and an introduction to the largest body of sacred writings in existence. Brilliant; needs to be read slowly. The author is the founder of the Friends of the Western Buddhist Order.

4. *Das Nibelungenlied.* The Middle High German epic poem. Richard Wagner derived much of the story and the poetry of his *Ring of the Nibelungs* from this long and intricate work. The writing is quite beautiful, but unfortunately it is extremely difficult to translate so as to keep the writing and the emotional content both intact.. This is one of the great masterpieces of German literature, from the era of high courtly love and troubadour (minnesingers) poetry of the thirteenth century, a distinctive style that does not appeal to everyone equally. Wagner's music is magnificent, but his poetry is nowhere near as good as the original (in spite of his very high, overblown, regard for his own literary skills).

5. The poetry of Walther von der Vogelweide, another medieval poet of courtly love. He was prolific, and his writing is exquisite. Even more than the Nibelungenlied, I do not know of any

translation that adequately conveys the beauty of his verse. When I first encountered these Middle High German works in college, I was transported and astounded.

6. Queen Marie of Romania: *Later Chapters of My Life.* One of the great characters of the twentieth century. Called "the most voluptuous queen in Europe," she was a granddaughter of Queen Victoria and Czar Alexander II of Russia. At the end of the First World War, Romania was on the losing side and was due to be severely punished. Queen Marie attended the Peace Conference at Versailles and used her beauty and intelligence to charm the Allied leaders into giving her country a much-improved settlement.

After her return to Romania, she was on very poor terms with her son, King Carol II, who kept her secluded as a virtual prisoner. He bought up all the copies of her memoirs he could find and destroyed them and then refused to let her publish this fourth volume, which was smuggled out of Romania and eventually published surreptitiously. Queen Marie was one of the few European royals who could write, and she wrote very well, as did her mother-in-law, Queen Carmen Silva, Queen of Romania.

She was eccentric and flamboyant. A friend in New York told me this story about his mother (Mrs. V.R., a New Yorker), a friend of the queen, who went to visit her in Bucharest. Queen Marie took them on a visit to her favorite residence, Castle Bran (fourteenth century), which had been the dwelling of Vlad Tepes (Dracula). One day they took an excursion to the nearby Black Sea beach. On noticing her strange dull black adornments, Mrs. V.R. asked the queen what they were.

Marie replied, "As a queen, it would be inappropriate for me to go out of my palace without wearing some of my jewels. But it would be foolish to wear my fine jewels to the beach, so I ordered several of them to be duplicated in black rubber, and here you see them." Queen Marie did not think this an odd or amusing situation. She had designed her own coronation robes. This book is charming, interesting, and well written. Highly recommended.

7. Prince Felix Yusupov: *Lost Splendor.* The Prince, a member of Russia's richest family, dressed as a beautiful transvestite, and

wearing his mother's fabulous pearls, attended a party in London where the King of England became overly interested in him, thinking he was a beautiful lady. An awkward situation was narrowly averted. He was married to the czar's niece Irina. Later on, as the leader of a small group of aristocrats, he murdered the dissolute monk Rasputin in an effort to avoid disaster and the collapse of the monarchy. Sadly, he failed to stop history, but he certainly produced a fascinating book.

8. Douglas Smith: *Former People, the Last Days of the Russian Aristocracy.* The heartbreaking account of the extinction of a culture and destruction of a class. We might all benefit from looking at this book so as to get a preview of what may be coming here as a result of the behavior and decisions of our rulers. The situation here in the United States in early 2016 reminds me of the situation in Russia in 1916 before the Bolsheviks took over, with an autocratic government; a generally incompetent, bloated, arrogant, profligate, irresponsible, and corrupt bureaucracy; and very little governmental interest in the welfare of the citizens, along with a tremendous discrepancy between the income of the poor and the middle class and the very rich. I remember the Great Depression, when people were proud of their integrity and their honesty, and even in being kind and considerate to their fellow men. These virtues are not very popular at the present time. Now, being tricky, untruthful, selfish, pretentious, and very flashy are often more respected. And knowing how to work the system to our own benefit and the disadvantage of others is the self-satisfied goal of many. That mode of behavior didn't work well in prerevolutionary France, or early twentieth-century Russia, or in mid twentieth-century Germany and in the long run will produce the same disastrous results here in the United States. The similarities are ominous and discouraging. "What fools these mortals be."

9. Bill Dedman and Paul Clark Newell Jr.: *Empty Mansions: The Mysterious Life of Huguette Clark.* Her father, the copper baron Senator W. A. Clark, was a man of immense wealth; at times, he was said to be wealthier then John D. Rockefeller. Huguette had the most careful upbringing and then a most unsuccessful short and unfulfilled marriage. She gradually became more retiring and then reclusive. Her

Fifth Avenue apartment, combined from three other apartments, was the largest in New York.

She had a magnificent estate in Connecticut and an even more palatial home in Santa Barbara. The walls in all three were hung with museums full of paintings, including many French impressionists. She was perhaps most interested in her immense collection of antique dolls and on a regular basis ordered huge wardrobes of clothes for them from Worth, Chanel, and other Parisian couturiers. By her own wish, she lived many of her last years in a small, private room in a New York hospital. She was not miserly or overly anxious and was generally very generous to her friends and various philanthropies. She just did not like being around people, but she had a few long-time faithful friends. Many of her servants, who had worked for her for years, said they had never spoken with her or even seen her. She established an endowment to buy flowers every day for her mother's mausoleum; when I went to visit there, a beautiful bouquet of flowers in an elaborate bronze vase was standing just in front of the mausoleum. Huguette's coffin was just inside the glass doors with gilt lettering. When she died at age 104, her fortune was said to be $300 million, and she still had a ticket for a first-class cabin on the second Atlantic crossing of the Titanic. Huguette's was an interesting and not melancholy story. I would have liked to have known her (probably).

10. Consuelo Vanderbilt Balsan: *The Glitter and the Gold*. An interesting and powerful woman, she knew everyone from the Czar of Russia on. This was an era during which wealthy parents were sometimes interested in marrying their daughters to European aristocrats, and the impoverished European aristocrats were interested in unions with wealthy American heiresses. For a while, Consuelo was married to the Duke of Marlborough, and as Duchess of Marlborough, she had heavy social duties. Winston Churchill was her cousin through the Marlborough family. She was in the same financial and social class as Huguette Clark, but their lives could not have been more different. I have a feeling that they might have liked each other and could have become friends. I used to see her (then known as Mrs. Jacques Balsan) occasionally at the opera, and she had a very attractive and impressive presence.

I knew a lady who was brought up in one of the wealthiest Middle Eastern families; she eventually had a marriage arranged by her family and not much to her liking. The couple stayed together their entire lives, and the marriage was somewhat turbulent at times. Sophisticated and thoughtful, she commented that in her opinion arranged marriages were about equally as happy as love matches.

11. Countess Elizabeth von Arnim; *All the Dogs of My Life*. She was born in Australia and later married a Pomeranian nobleman and lived with him in his castle in Pomerania. After his death, she moved to a chalet in Switzerland where she spent the rest of her life. She was in the middle of the European literary world and continued writing and publishing. She wrote *Elizabeth and Her German Garden, Enchanted April*, and *All the Dogs of My Life,*

This book is a charming memoir of her life and her dogs, most of whom, as everyone knows, are more congenial than most people. Toward the end of her life, H. G. Wells became her lover. There were others.

For the majority of the past fifty years, I have had the good fortune to have had the companionship of several gentle and loving canine companions. My current dog, Dixie, is a beautiful twelve-year-old wirehaired dachshund who has won several prizes at dog shows. She would have enjoyed knowing my previous dogs Sparky, Delilah, Rover, and Valentine, all wirehaired dachshunds. She often looks at me with intelligent eyes, and I wonder what is in her mind. She is very calming and cheerful company, and she improves the quality of my life.

12. Anthony Powell: *A Dance to the Music of Time*. An engrossing panoramic novel that takes place in England in the first half of the twentieth century. Wonderfully intricate and coherent. The end of the book, after twelve volumes, seemed to come too soon.

13. James Merrill: *The Changing Light at Sandover*. A very long poem, more than five hundred pages and incorporating many poetic forms. A cosmology, dictated over the Ouija board. These messages from the spirit world are very fantastic, dictated by various angels,

archangels, various disembodied spirits, and deceased friends of the author. Finely written poetry, which include some warnings about the behavior of the human race, with predictions of dire consequences. Could be. More likely all the time. James Merrill's father was the founder of the Merrill Lynch brokerage firm. The book is more interesting than you might think.

14. Charles G. Finney: *The Circus of Dr. Lao.* Dr. Lao's circus comes to town, bringing with it many strange and authentic sideshows, such as a real medusa who turns a member of the audience to stone and a fortune teller who really sees the future but hesitates to tell what he knows. Something of a cult classic, spotlighting in a humorous way the sinister nonsense of daily life. The book was made into a movie starring Tony Randall and has also been on Broadway. The author should not be confused with Charles G. Finney, the eminent Victorian mathematician.

15. John Kennedy Toole: *A Confederacy of Dunces.* A friend told me this was one of the funniest books he had ever read. This kind of recommendation usually suggested to me that the humor was dull and coarse, featuring sex, drunkenness, and football games—a big bore. But I took a chance. What a delight!

I agree with my friend. I laughed out loud all through the book. Unfortunately, the book was taken to a publisher by the author's mother only after her son, the author, had committed suicide.

16. Heinrich Mann: *The Blue Angel.* This was made into an outstanding movie starring Emil Jennings and the young Marlene Dietrich. Often thought of as the commonplace lurid story of the infatuation of a fat old school teacher for a glamorous cabaret singer, with the expected bad result. Actually, the story is much grimmer and more interesting. The professor and the singer meet and fall in love. He represents the respectability and stability that she longs for; she represents the sexuality and emotional freedom that the professor has always yearned for.

They marry, and for a while they are very happy. The singer has to travel in her work, and the professor quits his job and travels with her, eventually assisting her in the cabaret show and being put into a degrading rooster act. Each one, in trying to help and be close to the other, loses his most appealing quality. She loses interest in him and begins an affair with the show's strongman. The professor is brokenhearted, but in a jealous rage assaults her and then commits suicide. The conclusion is powerfully tragic.

17. Bram Stoker: *Dracula*. This is the most frightening book I have read. Bram Stoker was a master at creating mood and an atmosphere of horror. A few years ago I attended a psychiatric convention, and among the hundreds of lectures offered was one on vampires. I assumed this would be about how some people could drain the energies from others—psychic vampires. Most everyone has had this unpleasant experience. Sometimes I was not able to understand the mechanism and assumed the vampire was doing this unconsciously. But not necessarily. The lecturer, apparently serious and sincere, began describing a coven of modern day vampires personally known to him who lived in Chicago, practiced vampiric rituals, and actually liked to drink human blood. He told of a mail-order business that sold human blood for vampire consumption. I knew from my time in surgical internship that human blood is very irritating to the stomach and induces vomiting—not at all a fun activity for voluntary participants, even vampires. So what was I to make of the lecturer's presentation? I'll never know.

18. Mary Shelley: *Frankenstein*. The monster was brokenhearted that no one (except the little blind girl) could bring himself to be kind to him, because of his horrible appearance. He begged his creator to "fix" him, but his creator turned away from him in disgust. The monster was filled with a feeling of combined yearning, sorrow, and rage and vowed revenge on his creator before killing an innocent person who happened to be close by. The creator followed the monster around the earth, trying to catch and destroy his creation. They sail into the polar regions, and the boat becomes hopelessly stuck in the ice. The monster is careful to stay in plain view on the ice, but always out of reach, tantalizing the creator. Eventually, Dr. Frankenstein and the other humans starve and die. The monster goes on board the boat and finds his creator dead.

271

The story ends with the monster cradling his dead creator in his arms, weeping bitterly and forever alone on the ice. Some of us have had a similar experience. I believe Mary Shelley's work is a masterpiece. Whenever you may be in Geneva, look up at the flat-topped stone mountain, the Salève, just outside the city, where the monster was last seen as he tried to run away to hide and find solace.

19. Alice Miller: *Prisoners of Childhood.* This is a very clear description of the mechanism by which parents transmit their own pathology (or its opposite) to their offspring. Alice Miller, the Swiss psychoanalyst, is very convincing. As a formerly practicing psychiatrist, I can recommend this book highly to all new (or older) parents and to all who are interested in the persistence and spread of psychopathology, or who wish to understand their own childhoods better.

20. Robert Monroe, three books: *Journeys Out of the Body, Far Journeys,* and *Ultimate Journey.* Robert Monroe was a successful businessman and owner of television stations, as well as recording studios. He began to have spontaneous out-of-body experiences (OBEs), which at first frightened him. He further investigated the OBEs extensively and then wrote these three fascinating books about what he had experienced. Later he established the Monroe Institute outside Charlottesville, Virginia, to further investigate these matters.

He wrote of hemispheric synchronization, or bringing the two hemispheres of the brain into more useful contact, which might open new vistas of knowledge and understanding for us all. I enrolled for two separate sessions at the institute and had some truly unusual and interesting experiences. The institute and its books seem totally sincere and open, convincing without being proselytizing. This is not a religious organization and only requests that you may be open to the idea that there is more to us than the physical body. That is not difficult to accept.

21. Bhikkhuni Miao Kwang Sudharma: *Wonderful Light –Memoirs of an American Buddhist Nun.* She re-established the order of Buddhist nuns in Sri Lanka after an absence of one thousand years. A humble and very impressive book.

272

22. Music: all of these are piano music:
    a. Franz Liszt: "Benediction of God in the Solitude."
    b. Anton Rubinstein: "Rêve Angélique."
These two pieces are described in the earlier chapter "We Visit a Grand Duchess."
    c. Deodat de Severac: piano music. De Severac was a brilliant contemporary of Ravel and Debussy, and some thought he was their equal as a composer. He hurt his career by withdrawing from the musical life in Paris and retiring to his home in Languedoc. Listen to his music and close your eyes—and be transported to the south of France, with its miles of pink oleanders.
    d. Alexander Scriabin: "Prelude, op 11, #4." Brief (two minutes), beautiful, and very melancholy.
    e. Frederick Chopin: "Andante Spianato and Grande Polonaise Brillante." A wonderful example of the nineteenth century's brilliant pianism at its best.

Author in Hobart, Tasmania)

Russian church, Biarritz

Author in Liverpool, United Kingdom

Author at Versailles

Author at Guggenheim Museum, Bilbao, Spain

Author with friends Bill and Herb in Fort Lauderdale, Florida

Author in Milford Sound, New Zealand

277

Milford Sound, New Zealand

Rick and his aunt Mims

Candies in Istanbul

Steve

279

Chapter 21

Onward

Looking back over the eighty-five-plus years of my life (so far), I feel very blessed and incredibly lucky in so many ways. But apparently I like to complain. It helps greatly when I am feeling low or underappreciated. I am sorry if that is hard on others. My complaints are almost reflexive—just as when one knocks into a piece of furniture and then lets loose with an expletive—perhaps expressive but not significant. I don't expect anyone to listen.

Travel has been fascinating and surprising. I have visited many parts of our world, from Ethiopia under Emperor Haile Selassie to McAllen, Texas, and from Bora Bora in French Polynesia to Newfoundland and Buenos Aires, to the Serengeti plains with their millions of animals. All have been interesting and enjoyable (some places more than others, of course).

I have been surrounded by and have been a recipient of great love in my life, and I thank all my dear friends for this. And just as important, I have had the freedom to love others, with a few exceptions when my interest was not welcome.

Music has sustained me through many a hard spell. I have had the freedom to listen and play the piano as much as I want and also the freedom to think and read and use my own imagination. I once heard a lecture on the subject of "instruction and learning through the imagination"—an interesting matter.

Author's terrace, New York City

I am very grateful for a wonderful life, including generally excellent health. Now at age eighty-five, almost all my faculties are adequately functional, although some are not quite as effective as previously. In a life this long, there have been a number of health crises, some potentially fatal, but all manageable with the advances of modern medicine.

I look forward to many further adventures, both in this life and in the next ones too. The future is welcoming.

To all those who have read some or all of this memoir, thank you, and I hope it has been entertaining enough.

Parting advice:

1. William of Occam's razor: Do not multiply entities beyond necessity.
2. It is never too late to do nothing at all.
3. Don't punch time in the nose.

Author's terrace, New York City)

Just as this book was due to be published, a major change in the political and physical governance of the United States took place. As a result, there is a wide variety of opinions and possibilities regarding the future of the United States, ranging from a desirable and pleasant result to a catastrophic one, perhaps eventuating in the destruction of our planet and civilization. At the moment the author sees no clear likelihood of either result, but I hope we can continue to expect the future will be welcoming.

Good luck to us all.

Author in Queenstown, 2015

Author in Wellington, 2015

Made in the USA
Middletown, DE
27 June 2020